The Smokeweaver's Daughter and Other Plays by Thomas Barbour

The Smokeweaver's Daughter

The Last of the Mammoths

The Man in the Tweed Suit

Contradance

The Edge of the Abyss

I0159942

stage plays

contents

THE SMOKEWEAVER'S DAUGHTER

a comedy in two acts

The Smokeweaver's Daughter

The Smokeweaver's Daughter had been in the playwright's mind for a long time before he left for Europe to write in October, 1950, and his conception was typed down in Paris by the end of that year. In its original and somewhat shorter version, it was performed in the summer of 1952 by the members of Group Twenty Players, then a non-professional theatre organization based in Avon, Connecticut.

Later, an agent expressed some distress because, in its original version, the relationship between the boy and the girl was terminated. The play was expanded to its present form, suggesting a prospect of marriage between the two young people at some future date. Several more songs were then also added. In April of 1959, the play was produced in New York, Off-Broadway, at the Fourth Street Theatre, by the playwright in partnership with Charles Olsen, who also directed the production. The music[†] was composed by Robert Chambers; the set was designed by Charles Brandon, and the costumes by Mary McKinley. The cast was as follows:

> The Smokeweaver. . . . . Joseph Barr
> Ivy, *his daughter*. . . . . Irene Riordan
> Hollis Greengage . . . . Calton Colyer
> The Count. . . . . Frederick Rolf
> The Countess . . . . Ruth Maynard

cast of characters

The Smokeweaver

Ivy, *his daughter*

Hollis Greengage

The Count

The Countess

the action

THE ACTION takes place in the yard outside the Smokeweaver's house. One side of the house may be seen at the right of the stage. There is an entrance to the house upstage right; an exit leading off downstage right presumably is the way to the kitchen door. An open window, flanked by shutters, affords a glimpse of the room within, decorated with gay, feminine wallpaper; there are one or two pots of bright flowers on the sill. Stage left, there is a large tree with an exit downstage of it; the lower part of the first branch, in full leaf, extends overhead across the yard, almost reaching to the house. Under the tree are three stools and a rustic table. A hedge, far upstage, runs from the house to the tree, enclosing the yard. Beyond is a vista of mountains, green hills to the fore, snowy peaks in the distance, all under a sky of intense summer blue.

[†]The musical score for the songs in the play can be obtained by writing to the publisher.

Act I

Late afternoon. The SMOKEWEAVER *enters from the house.*

SMOKEWEAVER: Good evening. I've been called upon to say
    A word or two to introduce this play.

    I am the Smokeweaver – or I was until
    I felt I'd done my bit and had my fill
    Of what this multifarious world affords
    By way of compensations and rewards.
    When you've seen every country, town, and shire
    (As I have), then it's high time to retire:
    You've had enough of buffeting about,
    Your wind is short, your legs are giving out,
    And you can readily imagine Hell's
    Like living out of luggage in hotels.
    So I've come home: all roads have finally
    Led me to this green spot, this house, this tree,
    And this – this prospect to bewitch the eye
    Of massive mountains marching to the sky;
    Here, careless, I accommodate my soul
    And let the world roll where it wants to roll.
    Well, that accounts for me. The sharer of
    My bliss and of my fond parental love
    The sole proprietor is Ivy, who
    Was partner of my many wanderings too.
    She…

IVY *enters, excited;* SHE *has a toy – a wooden cup with a ball attached to it by a string.*

IVY: Look I got it in the cup! I can do it three times in a row!

SMOKEWEAVER: Ivy, dammit, you've broken the spell.

IVY: Oh, Father, you've not been at it again?

SMOKEWEAVER: Surely you don't object? You never used to.

IVY: No, of course not – that is, I didn't; but now it's different, isn't it? I mean: you're supposed to be retired. I'm not going to let you go wearing yourself out when…

SMOKEWEAVER: Nonsense, Ivy. It does me good to dabble a little now and again. Keeps me fit and supple. Look, I can still touch my toes.

HE *illustrates, not quite successfully.*

Well, almost.

IVY: *(alarmed)* Stop it, Father; you're turning all red!

SMOKEWEAVER: *(Straightening up)* Whew!

IVY: Now you've done it. You go right into the house and lie down. And take your medicine – a tablespoonful in a glass of water. It's on the shelf over the kitchen sink.

SMOKEWEAVER: You sounded just like your mother then.

IVY: *(Tenderly)* Oh, Father.

SMOKEWEAVER: She'd be proud of you if she could see you now. You're going to be a fine young lady, Ivy, one of these days.

IVY: *(Somewhat grimly)* One of these days.

SMOKEWEAVER: Don't rush it; it'll be here soon enough. Come on now: smile!

HE *pats her on the back and sings* †*"Smokeweaver's Song."*

> Come dame and maiden, man and boy,
> Put care aside and welcome joy,
> Enter the ring and pay your fee;
> What happens next is up to me–
>   Up to me.

> I gesture thus to cast the spell,
> Cry "Alacazam!" – and wish you well;
> There's nothing more for me to do;
> What happens now is up to you–
>   Up to you!

IVY *begins to laugh.*

SMOKEWEAVER: There! That's by girl!

IVY *throws her arms about him.*

IVY: Oh, Father, I love you. *(Abruptly changing her tone)* Now, go and take your medicine.

SMOKEWEAVER: Hoho! Couldn't weasel out of it after all. Well, I did my best.

IVY: On the shelf over the kitchen sink, and there's a spoon in the drawer of the...

Whistling heard offstage.

Oh, dear.

SMOKEWEAVER: *(Teasing)* Hark, do I not hear the mellifluous whistle of young Hollis Greengage, who, having performed his postprandial chores, comes now to pay his customary court?

IVY: That's what you hear all right.

SMOKEWEAVER: In that case, I shall beat a swift retreat.

HE *turns to go.*

IVY: *(In panic)* You're not going to leave me now!

SMOKEWEAVER: Far be it from me to discourage the exercise of that young man's devotions. Besides, I feel a little tired. Thought I'd lie down a while.

IVY: But you know how I feel about Hollis.

SMOKEWEAVER: Indeed I do, Ivy. But you'll learn, you'll learn.

Turning again to go.

Might take a little of that medicine too. A fine restorative.

IVY: But, Father…

HOLLIS *enters down left.*

SMOKEWEAVER: How there, Hollis.

HOLLIS: How are you, sir?

SMOKEWEAVER: Oh, pretty well, pretty well.

IVY: Father!

SMOKEWEAVER: *(To* IVY*)* On the shelf over the kitchen sink, did you say?

Without waiting for her reply, turning to HOLLIS.

Goodbye, my boy!

The SMOKEWEAVER *goes into the house.*

IVY: *(Furious and frustrated)* Ooooh!

Pointedly ignoring HOLLIS, SHE *takes up her toy. Humming to herself, with seeming nonchalance,* SHE *attempts to get the ball into the cup.* SHE *succeeds easily and is greatly pleased with herself – so much so that* SHE *is able to turn to* HOLLIS *and address him with some superiority.*

And what have you come for today?

HOLLIS: For the same reason I came yesterday, and the day before, and every day: to look at you.

IVY: Am I such a wonder then?

HOLLIS: Such a wonder!

IVY: Some sort of freak perchance? Have I two heads or alligator skin? Am I bearded, dog-faced, or curiously tattooed? Maybe I am the uncommon yapock, the one and only…

HOLLIS: I don't know what a yapock is; but if it is a kind of flower, a strange sort of rose perhaps, unlike any growing in my mother's garden or any anywhere in our valley, then that is what you are. Uncommon anyway.

IVY: "Yapock: noun; South-American water-opossum with webbed hind feet."

HOLLIS: Then you are not a yapock. I'm sorry I said that; I meant well.

IVY: Of course you did, Holly: you are always meaning well. But I'm afraid you are depressingly ignorant. Don't you agree?

HOLLIS: Ignorant? Yes, I agree. But there was a time when I was quite the wise one, so I thought. That was before you came. There was not a copse in our whole valley, not a cranny in the hills about us that kept its secret from me. I knew all the byways of the rabbits in the bramble and where the deer slept at midday. I could fill a pail of wild strawberries before ten o'clock on a spring morning, and I could find the fattest hazel-nuts in the fall. I could name a hundred forest flowers by their seedlings, before they had even blossomed; and I could whistle as many bird-songs, and the birds would answer me. I could milk a cow, break a colt, shoot a partridge on the wing. There was not a boy for miles around nor very many men who knew as much as I. I was a proud one, let me tell you, quite full of myself, until you came. Now you have shown me all my wisdom is bound by what we see here from your father's hill; and though it seems on a clear day that you can look out over there into forever, the furthest peak is only two steps down the road, the way the world is measured.

IVY: That wide world, Holly, is my home. I was born in it, brought up in it. With my father I have been... well, everywhere I suppose; while you, you've been sitting in a corner here...

HOLLIS: A very beautiful corner, all the same.

IVY: Oh, I agree with you. Don't misunderstand me: this is a very nice place. Not very exciting perhaps, but very nice. Just, just the sort of place for my father to settle down in the winter of his life. But I am in the spring of mine and just beginning – shall I say? – to blossom; and so for me this is a corner, and I feel like a naughty child at school who has been sent into the corner. All she can see are two plain, ugly walls meeting in front of her nose, just the way your precious hills come together – didn't you say? – but two steps down the road. Yet she can hear, in the world behind her back, the other children playing together and dancing, as I can hear in my heart's ear dancing in all the diamond ballrooms of the world. And how that poor girl in the corner would like to put on her prettiest party dress! With a captain of the Guards, an ambassador, or the only son of a very important duke, she would dance and dance and dance! Oh, dear.

HOLLIS: Ivy, I know just how you feel. Much as I love this place, I have learned that it is somewhere only and not everywhere, I used to wake up in the morning with such joyful expectation I could scarcely wait to put on my clothes and run outside to see what was new in my little world. And always there was something: a newborn calf or a newly opened rose; the chicks had hatched in the night, or snow had fallen. But now I find that, after all, these aren't such great surprises, and I lie in bed for hours, it seems, and let the sun go on while I wonder how it would be to wake up in another country where everything would be new all over. I've thought of leaving many times; only your being here keeps me still at home. But if you want to run away, to go dancing or whatever you like, you'll want someone to keep you company and carry your baggage and show the way and... well, I...

IVY: Poor Hollis Greengage! Show the way? Oh, my dear boy, I'm afraid it would be quite the other way around.

HOLLIS: Very well then: I shall show you to the lip of the valley – it's not an easy road – and you can show me the way from there. I should be a most willing and eager pupil, and I would gladly go to your school forever. Oh, Ivy, Ivy, I think I am asking you to be my wife.

IVY: No, Hollis, you are asking me to be your teacher. Now I am not, as they say in novels, insensible of your interest in me. I am very flattered, Holly; truly, I am. And as a token of my friendship toward you, I am going to give you a little lesson. It will by my last instruction.

HOLLIS: What is the subject of the lesson?

IVY: Women.

HOLLIS: Oh.

Ivy: I am going to tell you all about women so that, when you are old enough to ask one to be your wife, you will be somewhat more certain of what you are asking. Here is your desk. Sit here.

Hollis: Old enough! I'm five years older than you.

Ivy: Only four years older – more or less. Besides women mature much earlier than men; it's a scientific fact. Sit down. Now: there are two kinds of women in the world: those who become wives and those who become teachers. And any woman who wants to teach might just as well resign herself to perpetual spinsterhood, for no man, no real man I say, would willingly be a pupil to his wife. Men must be masters, Holly; that is the lesson of the world. Not by any right of men, but by the choice of women. That is why schoolmistresses are almost all old maids and all girls fall in love with their college professors. So when you ask to attend my school, though you flatter me, you are not making an acceptable proposal.

Hollis: If that is true, what proposal would be accepted? Ivy, I love you so!

Ivy: You must propose to be my master. But you can see the difficulty there: I am a woman of the world, and you are a poor boy in a corner valley. There is nothing I could learn from you, nothing at any rate that I'd care much to know.

Hollis: That does leave me in a difficult position: I cannot teach you; you will not teach me.

Ivy: A very unfortunate position, I'm afraid, if your interests are marital. The only direction you can take is a retreat, unless, of course, you want to remain where you are: lovestruck and – shall I say? – quite hopeless. That would not be very pleasant for you, and I think I should find it rather tiring for myself.

Hollis: No, it would never do. But retreat is no answer either. I shall have to find someone who knows all the ways of the world, who will give me lessons until I am wise enough and masterful enough to be your husband. Will you wait for me till then?

Ivy: I should think it would take a very long time indeed, and I can make no promises of waiting. After all, Holly, I am not growing any younger. Still you would do no harm to try; at least you would have something to occupy your time more profitably than gaping here at me. Perhaps you could find a proper instructor, someone with plenty of patience surely, someone like the Count, for instance.

Hollis: The Count! Now there's a fine example for your lesson: what sort of a master can he be with a wife forever telling him what to eat and wear and say? Answer me, who's the teacher in that family?

Ivy: The Count is, unfortunately, somewhat of an exception to my rule, but he made a regrettable error in his youth and married a lady with a rather advanced education and an unrecognized inclination toward a career. I imagine he is profoundly sorry he never let it materialize. Yet he is a gentleman of great wisdom and great charm; he knows the world, Holly, and how it goes. However, if you don't think he would be a satisfactory tutor, no matter; I rather think he will not be with us much longer.

HOLLIS: I'm very sorry; I hadn't heard he was ill.

IVY: Who said he was ill, you silly goose? He's... but that I'm not at liberty to say. Heavens, how I talk! What time is it?

HOLLIS: I don't know; I...

IVY: Never mind; it's late. Off with you; I have a very important engagement.

HOLLIS: But...

IVY: No buts about it. School is out. The interview is over, and you have stayed well past your welcome. You must go.

HOLLIS: Well, goodbye, Ivy.

HE *starts to go. Stops.*

What are you doing?

No answer. Pause. IVY *is putting up her hair.*

Who is it that's coming?

No answer. Pause.

Well, I'd better go.

HE *doesn't go.*

IVY: *(Sharply)* Hollis!

HOLLIS: Ivy, you are a wonder!

IVY: Yes, thank-you. Good-bye, Hollis.

HOLLIS: Good-bye, my dearest.

IVY: Good-bye. Good-bye.

HE *goes.* IVY *looks off expectantly. Nobody comes.* SHE *sighs deeply–*

Oh, dear.

Then sings: †*"Ivy's Song"*

>When will my true love come for me
> Lackaday, willy-wally, lackaday-dee
>To carry me over the bright blue sea
> Lackaday, lackaday-dee,
>Carry me off to his castle fair,
>Give me a bonny blue dress to wear
>And a circle of gold to crown my hair?
> When will he come for me?
>When will my princely love come
> Tantara, tantara, and rum-turn-turn
>With sounding trumpet and rumbling drum
> Tantantara, rum-turn
>To carry me off, his bride to be,
> and live forever happily
>In a kingdom far across the sea?
> When will my true love come?

The COUNT *enters.*

COUNT: Ivy, my dearest girl. I came as quickly as I could. What is the matter?

IVY: *(Diffidently)* Matter? What matter? Dear Count, how are you? We were just speaking of you.

COUNT: Who's "we"?

IVY: Young Greengage and I.

COUNT: Hollis? Fine boy, Hollis. But you haven't told me why...

IVY: Yes, I suppose he is representative of the finest native stock.

COUNT: The very best, Ivy. They don't come better than he.

IVY: *(Carrying on her own monologue)* But I'm afraid he smells... well, rather like a cow barn.

COUNT: Son of the soil, Hollis. Solid, dependable, honest as the day is...

IVY: And really depressingly dull. I am quite exhausted from trying to make conversation with him.

COUNT: I noticed you seem seized with singular ennui. *(Trying to change the subject)* This noon, Ivy, I received a letter...

IVY: Do you like my hair this way, or do you prefer it down? Down, it makes me look a little childish, I think.

COUNT: I prefer it down. This noon I received...

IVY: I shall let it down then, if you like. Perhaps it gives me an air of wild abandon.

COUNT: ...this letter. *(He produces it)*

IVY: *(Letting down her hair)* Letter? What letter, dear Count? There: is there an effect of wild abandon?

COUNT: Very wild. I quote: "Come instantly and save my life. Ivy."

IVY: What's that?

COUNT: Ivy, you strange little girl, what tricks have you been playing?

IVY: When will you see that your "little girl" is a woman who...?

COUNT: Perhaps when she stops writing silly letters.

IVY: Yes, yes; I confess to the letter. It was indeed impetuous of me, but at the time I wrote under very great pressure and could not phrase it less alarmingly.

COUNT: I am always prepared to save a damsel in distress...

IVY: Oh, you are very gallant, Count.

COUNT: And I have forgone my customary walk, which my wife wisely recommends as an aid to the digestion.

IVY: I am sure you would risk even your digestion for a damsel in distress.

COUNT: More than that, dear Ivy. But on this occasion I see the sacrifice is in vain: either the alarm was false, or the maid has found her own salvation. Perhaps your father can be teased into a game of checkers. Is he at home?

HE *starts to go into the house.*

Ivy: You're not going?

Count: I find it hard to resist the gambling instinct, especially with the prospect of your father as my opponent, though the Countess wisely says...

Ivy: Oh, do not speak of her!

Count: Ivy!

Ivy: "The Countess wisely says. My wife wisely recommends." How can you ever endure a woman's ordering your life?

Count: Of my many weaknesses, Ivy, the one I least regret is my incorrigible disposition to submit to women.

Ivy: Ah, my Count, how bravely with a jest you bear an intolerable burden!

Count: I think we have pursued the matter quite far enough.

Starting to go.

Ivy: No, no; you mustn't leave!

Count: What is it now?

Ivy: The damsel in distress.

Count: Still or again?

Ivy: Still. The alarm was not false, and the maid has found no salvation.

Count: My poor little girl.

Ivy: There you go again. Little girl! Little girl! How can I tell you of a woman's problem when you think of me only as a child. Go in and play your checkers; I shall keep my anguish to myself.

Count: I can't very well leave now. You must tell me what is troubling you.

Ivy: No more little girls?

Count: No more.

Ivy: Swear.

Count: I swear.

Ivy: Do you think me very beautiful?

Count: I believe you are quite conscious of the fact.

Ivy: I should like to hear your opinion.

Count: I think you are a very pretty little...a very beautiful woman.

Ivy: I do not look ill?

Count: A trifle pale perhaps, but...

Ivy: Then it is noticeable?

Count: What is?

Ivy: That I am dying.

Count: *(Alarmed)* Great heavens, Ivy!

Ivy: Dying of incompleteness.

The COUNT *bursts out laughing.*

IVY: Don't laugh. You mustn't laugh. I can tell you nothing if you will not take me seriously.

COUNT: But, Ivy, really now...

IVY: There are certain things in life one doesn't joke about. I should think a man of your age and experience would have learned that.

COUNT: True, but...

IVY: This is one of those things.

COUNT: *(Resigning)* I shall take you seriously then. I shall not laugh.

IVY: Swear.

COUNT: I swear.

IVY: I know that people say that I am spoiled. If what they say is true, then I am to be pitied more than blamed. I did not spoil myself. It is not my fault that I have seen the world and learned the lessons of the world, though I am not as wise as Hollis thinks I am, nor, for that matter, as wise as I would let him think me. If I were, then I could live here in contentment like my dear father, for I should have such a store of experience I should need no more and could live forever on the memory of it. But I was never graduated from the world; I went through grade after grade, yet when the diploma was almost in my hands, I was taken out of school and hidden here. If I had learned nothing, this valley would be my world, as it is Hollis's, and I'd be happy in it. If I had learned everything, then I should be my own world and happy anywhere. As it is I have learned only possibilities, and I am incomplete, unfinished. Happiness is completeness; incompleteness without hope of being completed, that is the greatest unhappiness of all, and I am dying of it a little every day.

COUNT: Just what do you mean by being "finished," Ivy? What is it you want to know?

IVY: If I knew what it was, then I should know it and there would be no problem. Yet, long ago, I learned a possibility, when I was a child, when I was really a child. In the city where we were living then, there was an older girl who lived across our street. She would seldom speak to me because I was too young; she was not very pretty, although she thought she was. Consequently I loathed her. Still I envied her fiercely, for she had a lover, a young man, who was so kind and so good-looking that I used to weep whenever I saw him because she was old enough to speak to him and I was not. One night when the moon was full, I woke to the sound of music, and, looking out of my window, I saw the young man under hers across the street, the moon shining upon him like a spotlight in a theater. He was playing an instrument and singing most beautifully. Soon, there she was at her window, looking quite lovely in the flattering moonlight. She threw down a rose, which he caught and held to his nostrils, sniffing it so passionately that I began to giggle, thinking he would draw it right up into his head. Then suddenly, before I knew even how he did it, he had climbed the trellis and was perched upon her windowsill with his arms about her and his lips against her lips. After a while, they disappeared into the darkness of her room, and I could see nothing any more. I waited for the young man to reappear, but he did not and the moon went down and all was dark and I fell asleep. Next day, the girl, whom I was prepared to loathe more than ever, was so changed I scarcely recognized her. She spoke to me with great kindness, and she laughed often, for no apparent reason at all, a laugh like little bells that was the very music of happiness. Friendliness and gaiety gave her such beauty as she never had before, and, far from envying her, I loved her; for her joy made the whole world joyful. Whatever happened on that night was a wonderful, beautiful thing, and that I do not know; that is what I want to learn.

COUNT: Oh, that.

IVY: Ah, I knew you knew!

COUNT: No, I... well...

IVY: How modest you are! And so gallant and charming – I was just telling Hollis – so wonderfully wise, but so unhappy, poor dear.

COUNT: Unhappy?

IVY: Yet you have borne your misfortune so bravely; but, don't you see, you have paid your penance for your youthful mistake, and now...

COUNT: Mistake?

IVY: I shall release you as you will release me.

COUNT: Release me? From what?

IVY: Dare leave your wife and become my master. Together we shall go back to the world, and you will teach me everything!

COUNT: Stop, Ivy; stop right there. I can't possibly go with you. I have...well, commitments; I've responsibilities; I...

IVY: I shall die! I shall die!

COUNT: Damn it, Ivy, what you want to learn you can learn as well right here.

IVY: Then you will teach me here!

COUNT: *(Aside)* Lord, what have I said now?

IVY: You will come tonight.

COUNT: Tonight?

IVY: Under my window when the moon is full.

COUNT: Moonlight and mandolins. I suppose I should bring a mandolin?

IVY: Oh, yes, yes. It will be so wonderful!

COUNT: It will be wonderful indeed if your father interrupts us. We are the best of friends, he and I, but his cordiality may have its limits.

IVY: You will not come until he is asleep, and when my father sleeps, earthquakes and hurricanes cannot rouse him.

COUNT: How shall I know when he is sleeping?

IVY: When my light is out, that will be the signal. I shall have checked; all will be safe.

COUNT: And if anyone else saw me, he would say, "That silly old fool" – if not something considerably less of compliment.

IVY: No one need recognize you: you will wear a mask. A mask would be very romantic and mysterious and exciting.

COUNT: A mask and a mandolin by moonlight.

IVY: A mask and a mandolin by moonlight! Ah, my love, my love! Until we meet again.

Blowing him a kiss, SHE *goes up the steps and off.*

COUNT: Lord, Lord, Lord. You sentimental idiot, what have you let yourself in for this time?

During this remorseful rumination, HOLLIS *re-enters, left, below the tree. Clearing his throat,* HE *startles the* COUNT, *who turns and notices him.*

COUNT: Oh, hello, Hollis my boy.

HOLLIS: *(Somewhat out of breath)* I was looking for you, sir.

COUNT: You were?

HOLLIS: Yes, sir. I didn't think at first that you would do, but then I reconsidered; when all is said and done, there's no one in these parts – except, of course, Ivy and the Smokeweaver – who is better qualified than you; and so I was on the way to your house, when I met the Countess walking, and she said that you might be here.

COUNT: Not so fast, my boy. Now, what is it I am, at least relatively, qualified to do?

HOLLIS: To teach me.

COUNT: Great Caesar's ghost!

HOLLIS: What's the matter?

COUNT: Shall I serenade you too? Perhaps I could fix a party rate.

HOLLIS: What are you talking about?

COUNT: Oh, nothing, nothing; my mind wanders at times when I'm upset. I'm very sorry. Again, please: what is it you want?

HOLLIS: I want you to teach me.

COUNT: I thought you said that.

HOLLIS: I don't think you quite understand, sir. You see: I want to know... well, if I knew, I...

COUNT: If you knew what you wanted to know, perhaps, then you would know, and there would be no need for me to teach you.

HOLLIS: Why, yes, sir!

COUNT: Aha! But as it is, you are aware only of possibilities.

HOLLIS: That's right.

COUNT: Meanwhile, you are dying – or, at any rate, suffering severely – from incompleteness.

HOLLIS: How very wise you are!

COUNT: Yes; so I have been told. Quite recently, as a matter of fact.

HOLLIS: This is the way it is, sir; I'm greatly in love with Ivy, and I have already, in a bumbling sort of way, asked her to marry me.

COUNT: Oho!

HOLLIS: But she will have none of me, certainly not now, though there is the barest chance that she may wait. You see, sir, I can walk not twenty miles this way and that way and mark out in little more than one day's time the limits of all I know. Once I thought it was quite a big space, but Ivy since has shrunk it to the smallest clod of earth, lost in the endless acreage of the world. She knows that world and you know it, but I am ignorant of it, too ignorant for her. She will not marry me until I'm wise enough to be her master.

COUNT: Nonsense, Hollis. It's simple arithmetic: one plus one. You're a boy; she's only a girl.

HOLLIS: Not she. Ivy isn't "only" anything.

COUNT: Hmm, perhaps you're right.

HOLLIS: She's a woman of the world.

COUNT: I've heard that. So, if I understand correctly, to make you acceptable to this wondrous, worldly, highly complex and enigmatic creature, I am to teach you the facts of life.

HOLLIS: No, sir; I know them already. The ways of the world.

COUNT: Same thing, my boy, but with marginal flourishes.

HOLLIS: I'm afraid you are not taking me very seriously; you don't realize how desperate I am, and how depressingly ignorant. Why, I don't even know what a yapock is.

COUNT: I'm blessed if I do myself.

HOLLIS: *(Absently)* A South American water-opossum with webbed hind feet.

COUNT: *("Taking" on this with a little laugh, then sobering)* All right, my boy, I shall take you seriously; this is, I might note, the second time within the hour that I have been taken to task for my delinquency in that regard. Seriousness is apparently the temper of the day: so be it. I believe I can diagnose your case and prescribe a remedy: a little zoology, a touch of anthropology, a bit of geography, a dash of this and that, and we shall have you as wise as Aristotle or, at any rate, wise enough to answer to the immediate occasion. I'll tell you what I shall do: I shall give you the run of my library. You may go down any evenings you like, to the number of four a week, and poke about there. Borrow whatever books intrigue you for closer study. I shall make a few suggestions and be on hand from time to time to discuss, if I am able, whatever puzzles you. In return, you shall help me occasionally in my garden, which shows a persistent reluctance to respond to any of my ministrations; your present knowledge – which is not to be deprecated, my boy – can be very useful to me there. How does the plan appeal to you?

HOLLIS: Oh, marvelously well, sir. I cannot thank you enough, but I can promise you the finest garden in the valley.

COUNT: Then I shall have some trouble thanking you.

HOLLIS: As for the books, may I start on them tonight?

COUNT: You may if you wish, but I regret to say tonight I shall not be at home, that is, not until rather late.

HOLLIS: Then, perhaps...

COUNT: I have a very disturbing duty to perform.

HOLLIS: I'm sorry to hear that, sir.

COUNT: A very perilous assignment.

HOLLIS: I hope no matter of life and death.

COUNT: I could share no other hope more willingly. It is, in a manner of speaking, an...an assignation.

HOLLIS: An assignation?

COUNT: When the moon is full, I shall be leaving the comfort of my hearth; masked and carrying a mandolin, I shall hie myself, as they say, to milady's window. There I shall sing a serenade, an original composition – adapted, however, from an earlier occasion. The lady will throw down a rose, which I shall endeavor to catch. I shall sniff it so passionately that, if you were to see me, you would think I was going to draw it right up into my head. Then, if I can negotiate the climb, I shall attain the lady's windowsill, from which precarious perch I shall embrace her somewhat ecstatically and press my lips against her lips. After that... well, after that, I haven't really figured out what I shall do; I rather hope that, after that, the lady will let me go home.

HOLLIS: Is it worldliness to speak so lightly of what I should find wonderfully exciting? How I envy you! I could never muster the courage for such an adventure, though I should think really it would hardly be perilous, not physically perilous, that is – unless the window is unusually high or the lady has a father.

COUNT: The window might be managed safely, and though the lady has a father, he is a man of infinite good nature and, more to the point, the soundest sleeper in Christendom. No, Hollis, what troubles me is... well, thirty-five years ago, twenty in fact, I could and did serenade ladies, climb to their windows, embrace them with extraordinary enthusiasm; and "after that" it was never a problem: it came as naturally to me as breathing. But when one passes middle life, one is inclined, if care is not taken, to develop what might be called a moral sense. Now I am fifty-seven and the lady, though in some respects rather advanced for her years, is not quite seventeen, and...

HOLLIS: *(Finally catching on, with some indignation)* Wait a minute! You wouldn't be talking about Ivy?

COUNT: You are slow, Hollis. Indeed, I am talking about Ivy.

HOLLIS: Moral sense indeed! I thought you were being serious.

COUNT: I was being very serious.

HOLLIS: Yes: I can have the run of your library, while you have the run of my girl – any evening you like, to the number of four a week! I may not be very bright, but it doesn't take much zoology to recognize a snake.

COUNT: That's rather strong language, Hollis, don't you think?

HOLLIS: *(Somewhat subdued by the* COUNT's *mildness)* I know; I'm sorry. But a point of honor is involved, and I think strong language is in order.

COUNT: Ah, where honor is involved, more than that is in order. Outraged lovers have been known to shoot their rivals, or at least to knock them cold with a well-aimed right to the jaw.

HOLLIS: I couldn't hit you; you're smaller and weaker than I am, and a great deal older.

COUNT: If I'm young enough and strong enough to go window-climbing four evenings a week, I suppose I'm young and strong enough to take my chances in a fist fight.

HOLLIS: I'm sorry you put it that way, sir; it leaves me no alternative. Put up your fists then.

COUNT: Tell me, is a knock-out blow very painful, or does one lose consciousness before one has a chance to feel it?

HOLLIS: I really don't know; I've never been in a fight before.

COUNT: Then this is a novel experience for both of us. Come on; I'm ready.

HOLLIS: Well, aren't you going to put up your fists?

COUNT: It seems hardly necessary, since you will probably knock me out before I have a chance to use them.

HOLLIS: But I can't possibly hit you unless you at least pretend to defend yourself.

COUNT: All right, I shall pretend, if you wish.

HOLLIS: I almost think you want me to hit you.

COUNT: Indeed I do.

HOLLIS: Well that's the most ridiculous thing I ever heard in my life!

COUNT: Ah, now it's I who am not being taken seriously. I told you I had my doubts about the rendezvous, and it occurs to me that this is the best way out of it. Ivy can't very well expect me to serenade her if I'm unconscious.

HOLLIS: Do you mean to say you don't want to go through with it? You meant all that about "perilous assignment," "disturbing duty," and so forth?

COUNT: Every word. It was all Ivy's idea, not mine; she can be very persuasive.

HOLLIS: But you must be mad to want to pass up such an opportunity.

COUNT: I told you: I'm too old for that sort of thing. And besides, I'm very happily married.

HOLLIS: That's not what I have heard.

COUNT: You've been listening to gossip, my boy. Just because my wife seems at times a bit demanding doesn't mean our marriage is an unhappy one. Let me give you a little lesson, Hollis.

HOLLIS: What about?

COUNT: Women.

HOLLIS: Oh. Again.

COUNT: There are two kinds of women in the world: those who get what they want by teasing and those who get what they want by, quite simply, asking for it. When you are young, the teasers are delicious: they flirt, they flatter you, they evoke your manliness and flutter before your alleged superiority; yet always they exercise complete dominion and have their way in everything without seeming to have insisted upon anything. As you grow older, though, the myth of man-the-master becomes more and more transparent, and you begin to sense a loss of dignity in forever being the teaser's dupe. Meanwhile her deceptions become cruder: she appeals no longer to your love but to your duty, of which no man cares to be reminded; her tears, which once were charmingly pitiable, become merely ugly and quite tiresome; finally she develops an array of maladies and vapors, which she marshals to her support at the slightest sign of her husband's defection and so puts a strain upon you that no man over forty can cheerfully endure. Not so the Countess. She has too much respect for me and for herself to resort to coy deceits; moreover, fluttering doesn't become her, and she knows it. As for her feigning illness, that is out of the question: she is – another point in her favor – perhaps the most obviously healthy woman alive. Therefore, when she wants me to do something – usually, you may have noticed, for my own good, not hers – there is no beating about the bush: she just comes right out and tells me.

HOLLIS: And you always give in.

COUNT: True. But I always feel I have the option to refuse. I believe, however, I am unique among men: my wife has never made an unreasonable request. Now have I convinced you I am neither mad nor joking when I say I have no interest in this affair with Ivy?

HOLLIS: I think you have, sir. My apologies.

COUNT: Accepted. Now let us get on with the business at hand. You were going to knock me out, as I remember.

HOLLIS: Oh, that's quite impossible now; my honor is no longer involved.

COUNT: You may still do it as a favor to a friend.

HOLLIS: It would be very difficult.

COUNT: Come, come, my boy; I insist.

HOLLIS: All right, then, if you insist.

COUNT: Shall I stand here?

HOLLIS: I should suggest you stand clear of the table, sir; you might cut your head if you fell in that direction.

COUNT: Right; it might be overdoing it a little. *(HE moves)* How's that?

HOLLIS: That's fine; and it puts you in a good light, too.

COUNT: All set.

HOLLIS: Perhaps if you would lift your head just the slightest bit more...

COUNT: Like that?

HOLLIS: Excellent.

Pause.

COUNT: Now what's keeping you?

HOLLIS: I'm afraid I just can't do it. Are you sure you want me to?

COUNT: Of course, my boy; it would be the greatest favor.

HOLLIS: *(Reluctantly)* Well, as a favor then: here goes.

The COUNT presents his chin, and HOLLIS winds up, with little enthusiasm, to hit him. Before HE can carry through his swing, the SMOKEWEAVER enters, up right.

SMOKEWEAVER: I must say, for a fellow about to strike another, you haven't a very fearsome glint in your eye, my lad. What goes on here anyway?

COUNT: Dammit, you've interrupted us.

HOLLIS: It was going to be a fight, but now I'm doing him a favor.

SMOKEWEAVER: A fight between my two good friends? What ever about?

HOLLIS: I was going to defend my – or really, Ivy's honor.

SMOKEWEAVER: *(Not seriously indignant)* Ivy's honor? My dear Count, have you been presuming on my friendship? What designs have you upon my daughter?

COUNT: None now.

HOLLIS: It was to have been in the way of an...well, an assignation.

COUNT: Hollis!

SMOKEWEAVER: *(Still not too serious, but with some misgivings)* Sounds very serious indeed. What sort of hanky-panky have I been encouraging by permitting you on my premises?

COUNT: None at all, I assure you. There was to have been a bit of a serenade tonight, but I'm not going through with it.

HOLLIS: He's too old for that sort of thing.

SMOKEWEAVER: I should hope so.

HOLLIS: And besides, it wasn't his idea at all; Ivy talked him into it.

COUNT: She certainly did, though I'm not quite sure how. First I treated her as a child, but somehow she had me swearing I'd regard her as an adult. Then I laughed at her, and she, somehow, made me swear to take her seriously. I protested; she said she would die; and the next thing I knew I was committed up to my neck.

SMOKEWEAVER: If she were any other daughter or I a different sort of father, I should never believe such a story, though you notarized it in your own blood. As it is, however, I find your explanation entirely acceptable.

COUNT: I am much relieved.

SMOKEWEAVER: *(To* HOLLIS*)* Since evidently you accept his story as well, what were you going to punch him for? It would appear he rather deserves condolences for having got involved in such an unwelcome situation.

HOLLIS: That was where the favor part came in.

SMOKEWEAVER: Favor?

COUNT: It seemed to me a good way out of the mess if Hollis could incapacitate me for a while.

SMOKEWEAVER: A rather strenuous solution, I should think.

COUNT: I must confess I didn't myself look forward to it with unmixed delight.

SMOKEWEAVER: And not a very sensible one either.

COUNT: How not?

SMOKEWEAVER: From young Greengage's point of view, that is.

HOLLIS: Mine?

SMOKEWEAVER: You have, I think, a genuine interest in my daughter; haven't you, my lad?

HOLLIS: I have indeed, sir.

SMOKEWEAVER: An interest that is perhaps more legitimate than the Count's and also – shall I say? – somewhat more desirable. No offense intended.

COUNT: None taken.

SMOKEWEAVER: Then how do you expect to ingratiate yourself with Ivy by flattening the gentleman who has her present favor?

HOLLIS: I never thought of it that way.

COUNT: Nor did I. Well, now I'm back where I started from.

SMOKEWEAVER: You're always too impulsive, my friend, snatching at the most obvious solutions and too readily despairing when they fail. If the first answer doesn't fit all the conditions of the problem, perhaps a second will.

HOLLIS: What would you suggest, sir?

SMOKEWEAVER: I don't know yet; I haven't the details, though I can imagine the general picture if it's Ivy's notion. Suppose you outline your commitment for the evening, in a sketchy sort of way, just to jog my mind a bit.

COUNT: I was to come here when the moon was full…

SMOKEWEAVER: Ah, yes.

COUNT: …masked and carrying a mandolin.

SMOKEWEAVER: Masked! That's it! Hollis can go in your place; she'll never know the difference.

COUNT: Splendid idea!

HOLLIS: But...

SMOKEWEAVER: Don't stand in the way of genius, my lad. *(To* COUNT*)* What was to be the next step?

COUNT: I was to sing a song beneath her window, with an appropriate accompaniment.

HOLLIS: There, that wipes out the whole idea. I can scarcely sing a note, and I certainly cannot play a mandolin.

SMOKEWEAVER: No matter: the Count will go along with you. He'll take care of the music.

COUNT: As a musician, when you come right down to it, I'm a little rusty myself.

SMOKEWEAVER: You will do. What next?

COUNT: Ivy was to throw down a flower, which I was to savor passionately.

SMOKEWEAVER: That will be Hollis's job.

HOLLIS: But, sir...

SMOKEWEAVER: Don't be foolish, lad; you can smell flowers as well as the next man. *(To* COUNT*)* Then what?

COUNT: I was to climb upon her windowsill and embrace her, still very passionate.

SMOKEWEAVER: Hollis again. That's the important part.

COUNT: And after that...

SMOKEWEAVER: After that, Hollis, you be a good boy and go home to bed. *(To* COUNT*)* I shall trust you to act as chaperone.

COUNT: Gladly.

HOLLIS: Yes, sir, but...

SMOKEWEAVER: You see, the right solution will present itself if you just approach the problem calmly; all you want is a measure of intelligence. This way you will be released and Hollis rewarded, while your jaw no longer is in jeopardy. Now that everything is settled, suppose we celebrate with a little drink. I shall be back in a moment with the elixir.

The SMOKEWEAVER *exits, up right, into the house.*

COUNT: Ah, there's a clever old fellow for you! I should have thought of that solution myself; the point is that I didn't.

HOLLIS: I don't much care who thought of it; the point is that it is altogether impossible and I won't go through with it.

COUNT: Hollis, my boy, why in Heaven not?

HOLLIS: Ivy is certain to recognize me when I kiss her, if she doesn't catch on to the trick long before.

COUNT: All the better if she does. It will raise you in her opinion; all her objections will be answered when she finds that you are as capable as she believes I am, to be so romantic an adventurer. Ivy is not interested particularly in me, or, for that matter, in any special man; her concern is not for the essence of the doer, but only for his existence in the deed. In her eyes, the act alone defines her hero. The man who holds her in his arms tonight will be the man who purposes himself to be her lover; that is the only man Ivy cares about, and his name might just as well be Hollis Greengage.

HOLLIS: That's a very interesting theory. I shall have to think about it.

The SMOKEWEAVER *re-enters with tray, decanter and glasses.*

SMOKEWEAVER: I have been thinking: will your performance tonight be open to the public – or rather to a select audience of one, to wit, myself? I should very much enjoy it. I could conceal myself in some convenient bush and shall promise to be quiet as the tomb. Of course, if either of you has objections...

COUNT: Personally I have none; but I regret your being present is out of the question: the whole business hinges upon your being asleep. Ivy is to check in your room, and if all is well, she will put out her light; that will be our signal.

SMOKEWEAVER: I see. Well, that settles it. Too bad.

HOLLIS: There wouldn't be much point in your hiding in a bush anyway, for there'll be no performance. I'll have no part of it.

COUNT: Hollis, you said...

HOLLIS: I said I would think about it, and I have thought about it, and it's no go. Your theories are all very nice; but no matter what I purpose myself to be, I'm still Hollis Greengage, and as a romantic adventurer I'm a wash-out. So there's an end to it.

SMOKEWEAVER: Come, my lad; you know what they say, "Faint heart never won fair lady."

HOLLIS: Then the lady's lost, and no one is sorrier than I am. But when it comes to faint hearts, there's not a fainter one than mine in the whole valley. Ivy is quite right: I could never be her master. Why, even in broad daylight, she makes my knees tremble and my hands sweat cold; but Ivy with the full moon shinning on her...whew! That would witch me for sure!

SMOKEWEAVER: *(to* COUNT*)* A sad case, don't you think?

COUNT: Pity. Pity. He seemed like such a healthy boy.

HOLLIS: Health has nothing to do with it; I'm in fine shape. I could confidently face a raging bull, but not Ivy by moonlight.

SMOKEWEAVER: Very sad. Very sad. I can think of one remedy only. Hollis, my lad, I have here a little tonic...

HOLLIS: Oh, no; thank you just the same: I never touch it. I have heard Ivy make some rather strong remarks about imbibing spirits.

SMOKEWEAVER: Ah, yes; my daughter is an advocate of moderation in all things – that is, for everyone except herself. But this is only a harmless little sort of wine. *(To* COUNT*)* You will have a glass, won't you?

COUNT: *(Accepting glass)* Thank-you. Your good health.

SMOKEWEAVER: Moreover, Hollis, it is of Ivy's own making.

COUNT: Quite delicious.

HOLLIS: Well, if Ivy made it…

SMOKEWEAVER: Of course, my boy. *(Pouring for himself and* HOLLIS*)* Let us drink to Ivy.

COUNT: To Ivy.

HOLLIS: *(Taking a big swallow)* Oof! It's rather strong, don't you think?

COUNT: Strong? Strong?

SMOKEWEAVER: It was meant to have been an unassuming kind of extract of fruits, but it may have got a trifle out of hand. Still, it's good.

COUNT: Think only of who made it.

HOLLIS: It takes some getting used to.

COUNT: Always better after the first swallow.

SMOKEWEAVER: Always better after the first glass. Are you ready for another, Hollis? You had so little the last time.

HOLLIS: Well, if you're sure that Ivy…

SMOKEWEAVER: Of course, my boy. *(Pouring)* You know, basically my daughter's views on liquor are very sound. The human animal is too beautiful, too delicate a specimen to be preserved in alcohol; it destroys the patina, the gloss, which is all there is to distinguish him from other beasts. I never liked a fellow drunk that I didn't prefer sober. I've met many men in the former condition, but only in the latter did they become my friends. How are you doing, Hollis? It isn't so strong, is it now?

HOLLIS: No, sir; it just took a little getting used to. It's really very good.

COUNT: Think only of who made it.

HOLLIS: I am thinking.

SMOKEWEAVER: Here, let me fill up your glass.

HOLLIS: Well, if you don't believe it will…

SMOKEWEAVER: Of course, my boy. *(Pouring)* There are exceptions, however, to every rule. I once knew a chap in Amsterdam, kept a bicycle shop. The drabbest, greyest little wisp of a man you ever saw. The only time you ever heard him speak was when you asked the price of an inner tube, and then you had to listen very closely or you'd miss it. Let me see, his name was Dirk or Hans or… well, something Dutch anyway. Willem, that was it. Not William: Willem – a Dutch name. He was such a quiet, spiritless sort of fellow, you could scarcely believe he was alive; you had to take the doctor's word for it. – Yes, Hollis?

HOLLIS: Perhaps I might…

SMOKEWEAVER: Of course, of course. *(Pouring)*

HOLLIS: It's really very good indeed.

COUNT: And not at all strong once you get used to it.

HOLLIS: Ivy made it.

COUNT: The finest little fruit-extractor in the world.

SMOKEWEAVER: Where was I? Oh, yes: Willem. He was sub-human, Willem was. He was sub-animal too, for that matter, a kind of vegetable in fact and of a low order as vegetables go. Rather like a mushroom or a fungus growing – no, not growing, merely existing – in the darkest corner of the bicycle shop. One day, however, Willem came up against a glass of Holland gin. I don't know quite how it happened; some medical students, I believe, were conducting an experiment, and...well, anyway, the transformation would have astounded you. Not that much of Holland gin *(Indicating about two inches)* and he was snatched from the vegetable kingdom and installed at least among the lower vertebrates. For the first time you could imagine blood flowed in his veins, and his grey little eyes assumed the beady brightness of a bird's. *(*HOLLIS *gestures and the* SMOKEWEAVER *passes him the decanter)* Here you are, my lad. Another glass elevated him approximately to the level of an intelligent chimpanzee. He began to move about the shop, making gestures of industry and uttering curious little sounds, incoherent but amiable.

HOLLIS: *(Dreamily)* "She walks in beauty like the night
    Of cloudless climes and starry skies,
    And all that's best of dark and bright
    Meet in her aspect and her eyes."

I read that in a book in Ivy's house.

COUNT: Incoherent, but amiable.

SMOKEWEAVER: The third glass made a man of him, just an ordinary man, but a living walking, talking, human being all the same It was at this point we discovered he actually could ride a bicycle. In short, he was entirely presentable. But they gave him one glass more – all in the way of an experiment, you see. That turned the trick: the instant he drained it, Willem was hoisted onto his empyrean, through all the stages of humanity and super-humanity, until he had only to reach above his head to touch the ankles of the angels. The years fell from him, and he seemed to gain both strength and stature before our very eyes. An heroic glow suffused him, head to foot. Not only could he ride a bicycle, but he could ride it without hands and did so, down that street in Amsterdam, crying at the top of his voice – in Dutch, of course – "I dare do anything!" Willem was the only man I ever knew who was infinitely more of a person when he was...

HOLLIS: *(As if coming out of a trance)* I dare do anything. I dare do anything. Ivy, the moon betrays you: you thought that it would dazzle me; it only lights me to my love. I shall climb up to your lips upon a moonbeam, and my arms will be a charmed circle, ringing round all your wisest witchery. I shall be master of the moon and you! Oh! Ivy, Ivy, Ivy, Ivy, Ivy!

SMOKEWEAVER: That does it! How's the faint heart now, my lad?

HOLLIS: Couldn't be stronger, sir.

COUNT: And you're game for tonight's adventure, Hollis?

HOLLIS: Oh, game as anything. I don't know what's come over me, but it's as if somehow I'd caught fire.

COUNT: Hear! Hear!

SMOKEWEAVER: Splendid! Perhaps a final toast would be in order; I give you: "The fires of love".

ROUND: (COUNT *first voice;* SMOKEWEAVER *second;* HOLLIS *third*)
Here's to the fires of love–
Burning, burning, burning–
Long may they burn!

SMOKEWEAVER: Count, I leave the young man in your charge – and the elixir. *(Giving him the decanter)* Keep him in this temper until moonrise and pray for his head in the morning.

COUNT: Come, Hollis.

HOLLIS: I dare do anything!

Interlude

During the foregoing scene the lights have lowered somewhat so that the departure of HOLLIS *and the* COUNT, *down left, and the* SMOKEWEAVER, *into the house, is executed in twilight. The stage continues to darken, now more noticeably, until the mountains disappear and the house and tree are but black shapes against a night-blue sky. Stars come out. Night noises: crickets and peepers. The moon rises, focusing upon* IVY'S *window, casting upon the house wall a fretwork silhouette of leaves and branches. High among the boughs of the tree, a bird, perhaps a nightingale, essays a note or two.* IVY *appears at the window, carrying a lamp, which* SHE *sets down. Her hair falls about her shoulders; as* SHE *looks out of the window,* SHE *is brushing her hair listlessly. The bird, pleased to have an audience, bursts into full song.* IVY *sighs, "Hmm!," which might be translated, "Well, isn't that nice"* SHE *sighs again, "Hmm?" This time it is a question, perhaps: "I wonder what this adventure will be like?" And again, "Hmm", indicating* SHE *has some doubts, or maybe only that it is time to see if her father is asleep; for* SHE *now departs, leaving the lamp burning in her room. The bird concludes its concert. The* COUNT *and* HOLLIS *now appear.* THEY *are both wearing domino masks, to which disguise the* COUNT *has thoughtfully added identical black cloaks and broad-brimmed, black hats.* HOLLIS *by this time is perhaps almost too well fortified by the elixir;* HE *approaches the window bravely.*

COUNT: Easy, my boy. She isn't ready for us yet. Get behind the tree.

HOLLIS *(aloud, as* HE *retires into the shadows)* Yes sir.

COUNT: Ssh!

IVY: *(returns to the window, sighs again)* "Hmmm!" *(meaning, "Everything is quite perfect!" She blows out the lamp)*

COUNT: That's the signal. Keep out of sight.

HOLLIS: Yes, sir!

COUNT: Ssh! Now for the serenade.

†*(sings)*
Once in a woodland where I strayed
I spied a wood nymph wary;
I asked her if she knew a maid
That should compare with Ivy.
She answered, "None,
Not even one,
Can quite compare with Ivy."

HOLLIS: Wary – Ivy? That's a terrible song; it doesn't even rhyme.

COUNT: The last time the girl's name was Mary; it rhymed then.

IVY: Is anything wrong? Speak louder; I can't hear you.

COUNT: *(To* HOLLIS*)* Get back where you belong.

†*(sings)*
I put the question to an elf,
A mermaid and a fairy,
Just to satisfy myself
No one compared with Ivy.
They answered, "None,
Not even one,
Can quite compare with Ivy."

I'm sorry I couldn't do better by you, but it's the best I could manage at such short notice.

HOLLIS: That's quite all right: it seems to be having the desired effect.

IVY: What's the matter now? Are you talking to yourself?

COUNT: †*(sings)*

So I've concluded that to roam
Is hardly necessary;
Why wander when you have at home
A pretty girl like Ivy?
For there is none,
Not even one,
That can compare with Ivy!

IVY: Ah, my Count, my only love!

SHE *picks a flower from the pot on the windowsill and casts it down. The* COUNT *beckons to* HOLLIS *and scuttles over to the house, where* HE *leaves the mandolin.* HOLLIS *comes forward to the* COUNT'S *former position, picks up the flower, sniffs it, sneezes a little.*

COUNT: *(To* HOLLIS*)* Put that down. Time to go up to her now. Here, climb up on my shoulders.

The COUNT *crouches under the window.* HOLLIS *climbs on his back, rocking precariously.* HE *grabs* IVY'S *outstretched hands to steady himself and draws his face close to hers.*

IVY: Ah, my love my... phew! What's this? *(Sniffs)* You beast, you've been drinking.

SHE *lets go of his hands;* HOLLIS *clutches desperately to the window ledge.*

Had you no courage, no chivalry to come here without first getting drunk? You dreadful, vile old man, get down this instant!

SHE *strikes him;* HOLLIS *gets down rapidly.*

Help! Help!

HOLLIS *runs off, leaps the ledge, and disappears behind it in the darkness.*

COUNT: *(On his hands and knees beneath the window)* Hsst!

IVY: Still there? I thought you had gone. Take that!

With careful aim, SHE *directs a flowerpot upon his head.*

COUNT: *(Crumpling)* Ouch!

The moon goes out.

CURTAIN

Act II

PANTOMIME: *The following morning. The hills rejoice under a clear blue sky. Brilliance of midsummer sun; everything tranquil, in order. The one blot upon this happy landscape is the* COUNT, *sleeping miserably on the ground beneath* IVY's *window.* HE *stirs, stretches, rubs his bruised head, blinks his eyes at the bright sun. Noticing the fallen flower-pot, in an idle gesture of tidiness,* HE *sets it upright on the ground beside him.* HE *looks up at the window above;* IVY *is looking down, indignant. The* COUNT *offers to speak, but* IVY *prevents him with a disgusted, "Humph!," and slams closed the shutters. The* COUNT *rises painfully, crosses to one of the garden chairs, slumps into it, his elbows on the table and his head in his hands. The* COUNTESS *now enters, right, sees first the mandolin, which has been left against the downstage wall of the house;* SHE *takes it and, looking up, sees her unhappy husband.* SHE *laughs, partly out of relief, partly in amusement at his ludicrous, albeit pathetic, condition.*

COUNTESS: What a pretty sight you are! Here's your fiddle.

COUNT: Good-morning, my dear.

COUNTESS: Good-morning indeed! Next time you go off on some mysterious mission you had better leave a forwarding address. "I'll be back late," was all you said; "Don't wait up for me." Well, I didn't, and you can imagine what a shock I had this morning to find you had not been home at all. I've been making a fine fool of myself riding up and down the countryside, asking at every house for my husband. No sign of you at Hollis's. No sign of Hollis either, for that matter. His family are quite worried about him. What's been going on anyway? Was he with you? Where have you been all this time?

COUNT: Right here. Or rather, over there.

COUNTESS: That's a fine place to spend the night! What sort of a host is the Smokeweaver, I'd like to know, to get you drunk on that dreadful elixir of his and then not offer you a bed when you pass out?

COUNT: I had very little of the elixir.

COUNTESS: A little of that goes rather a long way.

COUNT: It does indeed; but, truthfully, I had very little, and I was not drunk.

COUNTESS: *(Genuinely concerned)* Then you've been ill; you've had an attack?

COUNT: Well, in a manner of speaking, yes, I have.

COUNTESS: You poor dear, I think you have been overdoing things a bit. You're not so young as you used to be.

COUNT: I'm afraid not. *(*HE *sneezes)*

COUNTESS: And you've gone and caught a cold to boot. Well, old man, it's home and bed for you, with a hot toddy and an aspirin tablet. And no more late nights for a while.

COUNT: You're a very sensible woman.

COUNTESS: I have to be with you around. Come along now.

The SMOKEWEAVER *enters from the house, up right.*

SMOKEWEAVER: Good-morning, you two. What, leaving already when you've just arrived?

COUNT: I didn't just arrive; I've been here all night along.

COUNTESS: I don't know what you did to him last night, but now I'm taking him home to bed.

SMOKEWEAVER: What I did! How's that? Did something go wrong?

COUNT: Everything. Ask Ivy.

COUNTESS: Ivy?

SMOKEWEAVER: Now that you mention it, she was unusually sour this morning. Came into the kitchen with a face like thunder to announce the yard was a mess and I should go out and pick up the rubbish. Could it be she meant...?

COUNT: Quite likely she was referring to me.

COUNTESS: What have you done to Ivy?

COUNT: It would be difficult to explain, my dear. *(To* SMOKEWEAVER*)* It would have been nice if you had picked me up last night; I have nearly caught my death. *(Coughs by way of illustration)* Where were you when she started yelling?

COUNTESS: Yelling? Look here...

SMOKEWEAVER: You forget: I was sleeping. Didn't she give the signal?

COUNT: You might have pretended. I thought you wanted to be in on it all.

SMOKEWEAVER: My dear fellow, I can never pretend sleep. When I assume a horizontal position, it comes automatically and profoundly. A sign, I believe, of an unsullied conscience.

COUNTESS: Two seconds more of this cryptic conversation and I shall go stark mad! What have you two boys been up to?

SMOKEWEAVER: As you see, Madame, I am somewhat in the dark myself. Last night your husband and my daughter were supposed to have kept a tryst, but evidently something went awry.

COUNT: Evidently.

COUNTESS: A tryst?

COUNT: She was suffering from incompleteness and rather expected me to do something about it. *(Sneezes)*

COUNTESS: *(Sputtering)* You and Ivy...! Well, it serves you right if you've caught a cold. What a fool I was to sympathize with you! I must say at your age you should be ashamed of yourself.

COUNT: I... *(Sneezes again)*

COUNTESS: Sneeze your head off; you'll get no coddling from me. *(To* SMOKEWEAVER*)* As for you, what sort of a father are you anyway to pair your poor child off with this idiotic fossil?

SMOKEWEAVER: Now you're being too hard on the man, and on me too. He did last night a very noble and charitable thing. I am glad to have been, in my small way, an accomplice to it.

COUNTESS: *(Skeptical)* Charitable? Really?

SMOKEWEAVER: Yes: he was helping Hollis.

COUNTESS: I can believe that! Oh no, I know my husband too well. Whenever he goes tom-catting, he's in it for himself every time.

COUNT: *(Mildly shocked)* My dear!

SMOKEWEAVER: Every other time perhaps, but not this. I'm speaking the truth. Ivy inveigled him into a rendezvous.

COUNTESS: *(Unconvinced)* Uhuh.

SMOKEWEAVER: A rendezvous which intrigued your devoted husband not at all, but interested Hollis a great deal. I suggested, and it was so decided, that Hollis take his place, masked, you see, to facilitate the deception. The Count was to accompany him to provide music, moral support, and whatever other benefits accrued from his incalculably greater experience.

COUNTESS: Almost I am persuaded.

SMOKEWEAVER: I refer you to young Greengage for corroboration on every point. Shall I fetch him for you?

COUNTESS: His parents would be happy if you could. I've been to his house already this morning. Hollis has disappeared.

SMOKEWEAVER: Good heavens, no! Where?

COUNTESS: How should I know?

COUNT: Fled into the hills, I suspect. Maybe we should organize a search.

HOLLIS, *disheveled, appears from behind the hedge.*

HOLLIS: No need for that. Here I am.

SMOKEWEAVER, COUNT, COUNTESS – *expressions of surprise.*

SMOKEWEAVER: Well, well, my lad, where have you been?

HOLLIS: Right here sir. When Ivy hit me and began calling, "Help!" I ran and jumped over the hedge. Then I fell. Apparently I tripped on this *(Producing* Ivy's *ball)* and... that's the last thing I remember.

SMOKEWEAVER: I think it's time to explain all this hitting and hollering. What did you do to my daughter, Hollis, if I dare ask?

HOLLIS: Oh, sir, I didn't do anything. I didn't have a chance to. But we forgot to take account of Ivy's temperance. She discovered I'd been drinking and took rather strong exception to the fact. She slapped my face. Quite hard.

SMOKEWEAVER: I see.

COUNT: Then for good measure, not realizing he had left, she brained me with that flower-pot. Very hard indeed.

SMOKEWEAVER: Spirited girl, my daughter.

COUNTESS: *(To* COUNT *– entirely reconciled)* You poor creature, she thought you were Hollis.

COUNT: On the contrary, she thought Hollis was I. If I remember correctly, she addressed him as, "You dreadful, vile old man!"

HOLLIS: I'm sorry, I didn't do better by you, sir. I'm afraid the elixir wasn't a very good idea after all.

SMOKEWEAVER: Possibly it wasn't.

COUNTESS: *(Glowering at* COUNT*)* I thought that elixir might have been somewhere in the picture.

COUNT: I promise you I had very little.

HOLLIS: So he did, ma'am, but I had quite a lot. I thought it was just a harmless sort of fruit juice.

COUNTESS: They told me that story once, too.

SMOKEWEAVER: Still, my lad, it gave you heart, now didn't it?

HOLLIS: Oh yes, sir; but it's given me a head as well. I feel terrible.

COUNTESS: You poor boy, you look terrible. *(To* SMOKEWEAVER*)* Do something for him.

SMOKEWEAVER: Surely. Come on into the kitchen, Hollis. Have yourself a wash and a cup of coffee. We'll patch you up in no time.

HOLLIS: Thank you, sir.

The SMOKEWEAVER *and* HOLLIS *exit, down right.*

COUNTESS: Poor Hollis.

COUNT: Oh, he'll be all right. When you're young, you can take a lot of punishment.

COUNTESS: But his romance is botched up rather.

COUNT: I don't think so. Hollis is good for another round, if he cares to fight it. Fortunately Ivy doesn't know he had any part in last night's escapade. It's I who have lost her favor.

COUNTESS: *(This, and the subsequent interchange, quite tenderly)* Is that serious?

COUNT: With luck I can survive it. I'm afraid you'll have to put up with me for quite a while yet.

COUNTESS: I could think of worse fates.

COUNT: Really?

COUNTESS: Oh, yes; I'm not particularly demanding. Not any more.

SHE *sings* †*"The Countess's Song" – the* COUNT *joining in the choruses*

> Years ago, the man I'd marry,
> (So I said) would have to be
> No plain Tom or Dick or Harry;
> Such was not enough for me.

He must be a gallant soldier
Or a poet with long hair,
Or (I thought as I grew older)
I'd accept a millionaire.

Nothing less could be my beau–
Ah, but that was years ago!

Years ago, years ago!
Ah, but that was years ago!

Well, no soldier stormed my castle,
And no poet called me fair;
No one asked to be my vassal–
Certainly no millionaire;
But it really scarcely matters
(Now I take the longer view)
That my dreams were torn to tatters,
Since I fell in love with you
And I've gladly eaten crow
For what I said years ago.

Years ago, years ago!
Ah, what I (You) said years ago!

THEY *start to go, but are again prevented, this time by* IVY, *who appears at the doorway to the house, looking quite imperious and menacing.*

IVY: Countess!

COUNTESS: Oh, good-morning, Ivy.

IVY: Do I see you being kind to that horrid man?

COUNTESS: Old-fashioned of me, I must confess, but I've got into the habit of kindness to my husband. It was once quite the conventional disposition of wives.

IVY: When they had been wronged?

COUNTESS: Have I been wronged?

IVY: *(With solicitude)* Oh, you poor woman, you do not know.

COUNTESS: That the Count came here last night? But, my child, he...

COUNT: *(Aside to* HER*)* Take it easy; she mustn't learn about Hollis.

The COUNTESS *gestures acknowledgement.*

IVY: Yes; he came to serenade me.

COUNTESS: Ah, my dear, is that so horrible? A woman of my age must learn to face realities if she wants to find her life at all endurable. You're young and pretty; I'm old and fat; my husband is only human. When I married him, I knew he was no saint. I might have expected him in his declining years to achieve a measure of beatitude, but if the fires of youth still glimmer in his deteriorating frame...

COUNT: Now really...!

31

SHE *silences* HIM *with a smile.*

COUNTESS: *(Continuing)* I suppose I cannot begrudge his giving them vent occasionally. Besides, I find it not a little flattering – especially since he has decided to come back to me – that he is still able to give a young girl pleasure. I hope you enjoyed the concert. He had quite a nice voice once; and, while it has probably declined in power a little it might be said to have gained in mellowness.

IVY: The Count was very mellow, I assure you; but the concert was no pleasure. In fact, it was all quite disgusting.

COUNTESS: That is a disappointment. I had understood it was a command performance, too; he should have done his best for the occasion.

IVY: So he told you I had asked him to come?

COUNT: Don't perjure yourself by denying it, young lady.

IVY: I should deny it just to punish you, but I shall not spoil my reputation for truthfulness: I admit I did not discourage his coming.

COUNTESS: In that case you have little cause to feel outraged.

IVY: I have great cause, and, by your own logic, I insist you have been wronged. Your views upon your husband's fidelity – or lack of it – impress me greatly; they show you are a more generous person than I ever gave you credit for being. Indeed it would be flattering to you if your husband in his dotage were still attractive enough to give pleasure to a pretty girl. You are wise enough to understand the graces of one partner always reflect well upon the discrimination of the other. But the point is, as I have said, I was not pleased. Far from being the romantic hero I had foolishly taken him for, the Count was so inadequate to the occasion he had to fortify himself with strong drink before he could find the courage to take me in his arms. This apparently necessary recourse to a stimulant, quite apart from the unappetizing breath it gave him, was to me the grossest kind of insult. By the same token that his pleasing me would have flattered you, his abominable behavior only does you injury by disparaging your good judgment in having married him in the first place.

COUNTESS: *(Amused)* Now that's the prettiest piece of sophistry I've heard since I left college.

IVY: I shouldn't laugh if I were you; you only bring further discredit upon yourself. Rather you should redeem your reputation by thrashing the man quite soundly.

COUNTESS: *(Remonstrating)* Ivy, don't you think...

IVY: I think it would be a good notion if you were to beat him here and now. It would give me the greatest delight to be a witness. That stringed instrument there, the relic of his fiasco, might be an appropriate weapon.

COUNTESS: My dear child...

IVY: Kindly don't refer to me as a child.

COUNT: Oh, humor her, my dear. I want to go home.

COUNTESS: *(Resignedly)* Very well then. Bend over, you old drunk. *(HE does so slightly. To herself)* This all seems pretty absurd. *(SHE taps HIM half-heartedly with the mandolin on the behind)* How's that?

IVY: Not half hard enough.

COUNTESS: Like that? *(Hits HIM again)*

IVY: Harder still.

COUNTESS: There! *(Hits again – with same force)* You know, this is rather good sport. *(Entering fully into the spirit of the thing)*

COUNT: *(Alarmed)* Careful!

COUNTESS: Off with you, you dreadful, vile old man!

SHE *beats* HIM *off stage, left, roaring with laughter.*

IVY: *(Alone)* Humor me, indeed! I'll teach him.

HOLLIS, *in much better repair, enters down right, followed by the* SMOKE-WEAVER. HE *approaches* IVY *tentatively, while the* SMOKEWEAVER *stays behind to remain by the proscenium, right, throughout most of the ensuing scene, a silent and bemused observer.*

HOLLIS: Good... good-morning, Miss Ivy.

IVY: *(Very gracious)* Why so formal, Holly?

HOLLIS: I don't know. I had an idea this was one of your more formal days.

IVY: What ever gave you that notion?

HOLLIS: Nothing, I suppose, but... You are not angry then?

IVY: At you, Holly dear? Of course not.

HOLLIS: But you are at...?

IVY: Let's not talk about that for a moment. I say I am not angry at you.

HOLLIS: I'm glad to hear that, Ivy.

IVY: In fact I am rather ashamed of myself for having treated you so badly of late.

HOLLIS: Really? I mean: you haven't treated me so badly, Ivy.

IVY: Oh yes, I have, my dear; and I owe you more apologies than I can say. Since we met last, I have learned a new lesson that has quite changed my entire attitude. I have learned that a man of the world may be a fool after all and the years that should have brought him wisdom and experience may only have robbed him of what little sense he had. I was deluded by the gestures of civility and the surface show of worldly etiquette, for I have seen how, in a crisis, these desert the man of little character and reveal him as he really is, vulgar, unmannerly, and base. Since I have had to revise my judgment of a gentleman, what shall I have to say now of my poor country boy?

HOLLIS: That he is a still greater fool, more base, more vulgar?

IVY: I rather think not, Holly. If I have been deceived in one case by appearances, could I not also be mistaken in the other? Although you do not dress very elegantly and much of the time your hair wants combing and your fingernails are not always so clean as they might be, you have a kind of – shall I say? – rugged charm, which may somewhat compensate for these deficiencies. That you are not wise in the ways of the world may not mean that you are weak of intellect. You told me once how you prepared the carcass of a deer you had shot, with many details I confess I found rather revolting, but I realize now this act required quite a deal of skill and knowledge which must be very useful in the life to which fate has assigned you and may even be almost as important as knowing how to converse politely, when to tip your hat, and what arm to give a lady. If you have not manners, you may yet be a man.

HOLLIS: Does that mean I have a chance then, Ivy?

IVY: It may well be; I don't know. Today I am jumping to no conclusions. I should like to think, however, that for all your faults you have integrity, that for all your apparent lack of respectability you still have self-respect, and that for all your bumblings and confusions you are motivated by a love for me as deep as it is incoherent, for all its awkwardness sincere.

HOLLIS: On that last point, anyway, you're so right to think so. Oh, Ivy, how can I prove my love for you?

IVY: You wish to prove it?

HOLLIS: I do. Indeed I do.

IVY: Well, in that case... *(To* SMOKEWEAVER*)* Father, instead of standing there and grinning at what should have been a private conversation, will you do me the favor of fetching back the Count.

HOLLIS: What do you want him for?

IVY: *(Ignoring* HOLLIS*)* If you hurry you can overtake him before he reaches home. He left that way *(Indicating)* not long ago. The Countess is with him. She might come too; I think she would be quite interested in Hollis's trial.

SMOKEWEAVER: Now, Ivy, take it easy. The Count is very tired.

IVY: I should think he would be, but I also think the information is immaterial.

SMOKEWEAVER: And he's caught a rather severe cold.

IVY: Under the circumstances, I should not care if he had pneumonia.

SMOKEWEAVER: And furthermore, in my opinion, you have been catered to just about enough.

IVY: You need not cater to me if you feel that way about it. Cater to Hollis rather. You're always telling me what a fine young man be is: don't stand now in the way of his proving it.

SMOKEWEAVER: For some months he has been proving himself to you daily, and you have consistently paid no attention to him. If you have managed to go all this time without accepting his proofs, you can surely wait for them till tomorrow.

IVY: I don't know what mood I shall be in tomorrow. Holly's best chance is now. Will you deny him it?

SMOKEWEAVER: You're talking nonsense, Ivy.

HOLLIS: I don't like to interfere, but I should hate to miss my opportunity. Please don't anger her: fetch the Count for whatever she wishes. I know it's asking a lot of him, but he will have the good nature to forgive us.

SMOKEWEAVER: *(Touched)* Very well, my lad.

HE *exits, left.*

IVY: You speak very kindly of the Count. That is strange if you know what happened last night. And I gathered that you knew.

HOLLIS: I have an idea.

IVY: Though I can't imagine who told you. Perhaps the Count himself was brazen enough to crow about it.

HOLLIS: He didn't crow, but he gave a rough outline of what happened. He had to in order to explain his presence here this morning.

IVY: I'll bet it was a rough outline all right. Maybe you should hear my side of the story before you start being charitable to the Count.

HOLLIS: I heard... or rather, I can imagine your side of the story.

IVY: It doesn't seem to have much affected you. I think you owe me an explanation of your indifference.

HOLLIS: I am not indifferent, Ivy. I spoke only of the Count's good nature because I have never seen him out of humor. He has always been very cordial to me; so I find it difficult to think angrily of him.

IVY: Hollis, the Count has not been cordial to me, and that should be sufficient cause for your being very angry. If you really loved me, you would know that any injury I received was automatically an injury to you.

HOLLIS: But have you been injured, Ivy? What harm now has the Count really done?

IVY: What harm has he done? I shall tell you what harm he has done: directly he has offended my senses, indirectly he has disparaged my attractiveness, and in every way he has ruined what was to have been the most beautiful evening of my life.

She bursts into tears.

HOLLIS: *(HIS arm about her)* There, there, Ivy my dearest.

IVY: So you see: if you love me, you cannot help but be angry at the Count.

HOLLIS: Very well, my dear, I shall be quite angry.

IVY: *(Brightening)* Really? Swear.

HOLLIS: I swear.

IVY: *(Remarkably dry-eyed)* Good. Now you are prepared to prove your love.

HOLLIS: Haven't I done that already?

IVY: But, of course not. That was only the beginning.

HOLLIS: Oh.

THE SMOKEWEAVER'S DAUGHTER

IVY: I have been denied one romantic adventure; you shall provide me with another. It will be proof of both your love and your anger.

HOLLIS: There's nothing very angry about a serenade.

IVY: Not a serenade this time. Something quite different.

HOLLIS: What?

IVY: I shall tell you. There was a girl once, a young lady rather, in a city where we used to live. I cannot say she was a friend of mine because she was a great deal older than I, who was then scarcely more than a child. She was very dignified and honorable and pure, but she was not exceptionally pretty. Consequently we girls, my playmates and myself, were able to admire her greatly without feeling envy in the least. She had a lover, a young lieutenant, whom we thought handsome enough, but rather dull until one day he did a very wonderful and beautiful thing, which made us all, when we heard of it, fall in love with him immediately and feel very envious of his lady friend indeed.

HOLLIS: What did he do, Ivy?

IVY: Apparently another man in the town, a man of rather sinister reputation did something very unpleasant to this girl. We were never told just what, but we understood he kissed her or something when he was quite drunk. The girl, who was very pure indeed, was naturally much offended, but her lieutenant rose to the occasion marvelously and challenged the other man to a duel, and...

HOLLIS: Hold on a moment, Ivy. You're not suggesting...?

IVY: Suggesting what?

HOLLIS: That I fight a duel?

IVY: That is exactly what I am suggesting.

HOLLIS: With the Count?

IVY: With the Count.

HOLLIS: But I can't conceivably do that!

IVY: Why not, Holly?

HOLLIS: The Count is my friend.

IVY: Really now! I thought you swore to me...

HOLLIS: No, I don't mean that. I mean... well, I just don't know how to fight a duel.

IVY: You said once you could shoot a partridge on the wing?

HOLLIS: I can do that, but...

IVY: Then you can shoot a Count standing still.

HOLLIS: But the law: I don't think this is the season for Counts.

IVY: Love and honor know no season, Hollis. As for the law, I don't recall that it gave the lieutenant much concern.

HOLLIS: At least let me consult some authority.

IVY: If you love me, Holly, you need consult no higher authority than your heart. But I do not think you love me after all.

HOLLIS: Oh, I do. I do.

IVY: You will not prove it.

HOLLIS: I will prove it. Tomorrow.

IVY: Today, Holly.

HOLLIS: *(Miserably)* All right then: today.

IVY: Good. *(Suddenly becoming very coy)* You know, Holly: you have very soulful eyes.

HOLLIS: Soulful?

IVY: Yes. *(Pats his cheek coquettishly)* Rather like a poodle's.

HOLLIS: I'm sorry, Ivy.

IVY: Oh, there's nothing to be sorry about, Holly; I like poodle eyes.

HOLLIS: I'm glad to hear that. *(HE hesitates)* Look, Ivy, I...

IVY: And you have dimples when you smile.

HOLLIS: *(Embarrassed)* Now, you're making me blush. *(Trying to change the subject)* ...er...

IVY: Blushing becomes you, Holly.

HOLLIS: Ivy, please.

IVY: Yes?

HOLLIS: Will you grant me one favor, a sort of payment in advance?

IVY: What, Holly?

HOLLIS: Kiss me.

   SHE *does so. Voices are heard off left.*

IVY: *(Breaking away)* They're coming. Now's your opportunity.

   The SMOKEWEAVER *enters, followed by the* COUNTESS *and the* COUNT. HE *begins to speak, but is immediately distracted by* HOLLIS, *who beckons* HIM *over, far down right. The* SMOKEWEAVER *crosses to* HIM.

COUNTESS: What do you want of us now, young lady?

COUNT: Yes, Ivy. I should be in bed.

   HIS *cold is evidently not much better.*

IVY: *(Pointedly ignoring the* COUNT*)* Ah, Countess, do sit down. You will see presently.

   Greeting the COUNTESS *thus with some ceremony,* IVY *offers her a stool at the right of the table and, seating herself at the* COUNTESS'S *left, begins to converse elegantly, in the manner of a dowager receiving at a garden party. The* COUNTESS *is puzzled at first, but as* IVY *begins to relax, the two of them proceed to chat animatedly about whatever women talk about when they are even remotely associated with a tea-table. The* COUNT *meanwhile edges himself into the remaining seat, left, and is resting peacefully until* HE *has occasion to blow his nose with some violence.* IVY *glares at* HIM, *and* HE *apologetically removes himself and his stool to a position downstage of the tree, where* HE *sits staring moodily off. During the foregoing pantomime,* HOLLIS *and the* SMOKEWEAVER *are downstage right conversing in undertones as follows:*

HOLLIS: I just wanted to say good-bye, sir.

SMOKEWEAVER: Good-bye?

HOLLIS: Ivy kissed me. At least I shall die happily.

SMOKEWEAVER: *(Disturbed)* What's this about dying, Hollis?

HOLLIS: She wants me to fight a duel with the Count.

SMOKEWEAVER: A duel, eh?

HOLLIS: I shall let him kill me, of course.

SMOKEWEAVER: You'll do nothing of the kind.

HOLLIS: But he's my friend.

SMOKEWEAVER: You shoot the Count, my lad. It'll be all right. I'll fix everything.

HOLLIS: *(Bitterly)* You fixed everything last night.

IVY: What are you doing, Holly? We're waiting.

COUNT: *(Coming to)* Waiting for what?

IVY: You'll see.

SMOKEWEAVER: *(Aside to* HOLLIS*)* Trust me, Hollis.

IVY: Holly, do you love me?

SMOKEWEAVER: *(Aside to* HOLLIS*)* Show her, my lad.

HOLLIS: *(Aside)* I wish I had some of the elixir.

SMOKEWEAVER: *(Aside)* It would spoil your aim. Go on: challenge him.

HOLLIS: Yes, sir. *(To* COUNT, *in full voice but faltering)* Count... sir...

COUNT: Yes, my boy.

HOLLIS: I'm afraid I must... that is, Ivy says... *(Furtively looks at* IVY, *who glares at* HIM*)* I mean: I challenge you, sir, to a duel.

SMOKEWEAVER: *(Promptly)* I'll go and get my pistols.

COUNTESS: What!

SHE *rises in panic and comes down toward* HOLLIS. *The* SMOKEWEAVER *intercepts* HER *and whispers something in her ear, at which* SHE *smiles with broad approval. The* SMOKEWEAVER *goes up the steps into the house.*

COUNT: Did I hear you correctly, Hollis? You want to...er... shoot it out with me?

HOLLIS: *(Amiably)* If you please, sir.

IVY: You're not being very aggressive, Holly.

COUNT: Will you answer an idle question, my boy: is it just possible that Ivy is behind all this?

HOLLIS: She has been injured, sir, directly, indirectly, in fact in every way, and, apparently, you're the one who did it.

COUNT: And so she has got you to challenge me to a duel?

IVY: *(To* HOLLIS, *sharply)* Don't answer that.

COUNT: I see. *(To* COUNTESS, *despairingly)* What shall I do now?

COUNTESS: Humor her, my dear.

COUNT: You're a help. *(The* COUNTESS *laughs)*

IVY: I don't know what you find so amusing. Your honor is at stake as well as mine.

COUNT: Ivy's right. There's nothing amusing about this; it's a very serious matter.

IVY: I'm glad you see it in the proper light. Well, do you accept Hollis's challenge?

HOLLIS: Perhaps the Count would like a day to think it over.

IVY: He can make up his mind right now. Count, I appeal to your last shred of chivalry, which must lodge in the breast of even the basest man. You have shown yourself an unworthy lover; will you now stand in the way of Holly's proving his merit?

HOLLIS: If you'd like to postpone the duel until tomorrow, sir, it would be quite agreeable to me.

IVY: I should not find it at all agreeable.

COUNT: Look here, Ivy. I don't think you understand the full implication of a duel. Someone is very likely to be hurt.

IVY: Are you afraid?

COUNT: Not altogether for myself. Hollis may be as easily hurt as I.

IVY: I hardly think that.

COUNT: I shouldn't be too sure, young lady. In my time, I have been reckoned quite a handy shot. There's a drawer full of medals at home to prove it.

COUNTESS: He's right. In fact he was known affectionately in his youth as "Kid Keen-Eye, the Continental Killer."

COUNT: And I'm sure I could kill a man today, if I put my mind to it.

IVY: *(Horrified)* Kill a man! Who said anything about killing?

COUNT: When two men fire pistols at each other at twenty paces, very often one of them fetches up quite dead.

HOLLIS: That's true, Ivy.

COUNTESS: You might say it was an occupational hazard among duelists.

IVY: Oh, that's not the kind of duel I want at all.

COUNT: I assure you I know of no other.

IVY: I only wanted Holly to prove his love and avenge my honor. When he had done that, we could all live happily ever after.

COUNT: You've been reading too many books, my child. Duels don't work out that way in real life.

IVY: I've sure neither of you wants to be a murderer.

COUNT: I'm sure of that too. But if I decide to accept young Greengage's challenge, I promise you I shall make every effort to effect his quietus before he has a chance to do the same to me. And you will try to do the same, of course, won't you, Hollis?

HOLLIS: Well, I... *(The* COUNT *winks at him)* Yes, sir.

COUNT: I don't imagine you are so vindictive, Ivy, that you would wish to see even me, as they say, cold in death; and I am certain you would especially not like it if Hollis...

IVY: Oh, no!

COUNT: I say, if Hollis were cut down in the prime of his manhood and left to expire languidly in your consoling arms.

IVY: *(Dreamily contemplating the vision)* It would be rather romantic.

HOLLIS: *(Profoundly shocked)* Great heavens, Ivy!

COUNT: The picture has its tender aspects, I confess; but there is about it an air of finality that quite takes the edge off the romance.

IVY: True, there is.

COUNT: In fact, it's not really, when you come to think of it, a very pretty picture at all: the pallor of his skin, the rattle in his throat, the ice creeping relentlessly into his veins, his gore befouling the unhappy ground.

IVY: No, no, no, no; it's horrible!

COUNTESS: Stop it; you're frightening the poor child.

COUNT: I was doing my best to.

The SMOKEWEAVER *re-enters, carrying a brace of pistols.*

SMOKEWEAVER: Here they are. Choose your weapon, gentlemen. *(To* COUNT*)* You've accepted the challenge, of course?

COUNT: As a matter of fact...

SMOKEWEAVER: I picked these up in Bolivia after a revolution. Quite a fine pair. Went very cheap. No more use for them I suppose: everybody'd killed everybody else. Here, try that one for size. Careful: it's loaded *(Undertone to* COUNT*, handing* HIM *a pistol)* with blanks. *(The* COUNT *acknowledges receipt of this information, clearing his throat)*

COUNT: Actually I had not as yet accepted, but I do so now.

SMOKEWEAVER: Splendid! Here's one for you, my lad.

HOLLIS *gingerly accepts the remaining pistol.*

IVY: No, no: you can't.

COUNT: Ah yes, I can, Ivy. I have made up my mind. I disappointed you last night; I shall not disappoint you again today. You wanted a duel, and you shall have one.

IVY: But not that kind. Oh, Father, make them stop it.

SMOKEWEAVER: I'm afraid the matter is out of my hands. Once the challenge has been offered and accepted, there's little I can do about it. Why are you upset, my child? They are doing this only for your pleasure. For some time now, you have had four grown people risking their sleep, their health, their necks, and their dignity to dance attendance upon you. Why? I don't know; perhaps because you have the weird and wonderful way of youth about you that makes all adults turn themselves into fools to do you reverence, since we old ones cannot help lavishing an envious devotion upon you young. But you must have charity when we can't keep pace with your quicksilver tempers, your alterations, and your moods. We are doing the best we can within our small capacities. The Count and Hollis, I believe, have reached the point where they are willing to satisfy your desire for a duel. I understand that these two worthy gentlemen are prepared to act only for the diversion and delight of my most precious daughter, and, by Jupiter, I shall do nothing to prevent them.

IVY: Oh dear, oh dear.

HOLLIS: Really, sir, I think Ivy has quite changed her mind about the duel, and I am more than willing and entirely able to keep pace with her in that alteration.

SMOKEWEAVER: After I have made such a pretty speech upon the subject, heaven and earth, Hollis, could not reverse my judgment. *(Softly)* Go along with it, my lad; I promise you all will be well.

COUNT: *(To* COUNTESS, *extravagantly)* My love, if I survive not this day's sun, weep for me tonight but think of me with joy upon the morrow; for I shall have died in the interest of your honor and that of our most dear, our mutual friend, Miss Ivy.

COUNTESS: I shall think of you.

IVY: My God! How can you take it so calmly?

COUNTESS: Ivy, the Count and I have shared a long and happy life together. Though I might wish to have him with me a while longer, I take comfort in the fact that, if he leaves me today, he will not have petered out in tiresome senility, but will have made his exit in full possession of his faculties, so to speak, with a bang.

HOLLIS: And Ivy, if the Count's aim is as good as I'm afraid it might be, will you think of me sometimes and how much I should have liked to have seen the world with you. And will you accept my dying as proof of my very deep and never changing love?

IVY: *(HER voice weak with emotion)* I will, Holly. Oh, I shall die; I know I shall!

SMOKEWEAVER: Are you ready, gentlemen?

COUNT: Ready.

HOLLIS: Yes, sir.

SMOKEWEAVER: Then, to your places. And may the best man win.

IVY: *(Closing her eyes tightly and stopping her ears)* I can't look.

SMOKEWEAVER: All set, Hollis? Ten paces, turn, and fire. *(Aside to* COUNT*)* And you: fall gracefully. Go to it, gentlemen.

THE DUEL: *They pace to opposite sides of the stage.* HOLLIS *turns, still averting his eyes, and aims in the general direction of the* COUNT. *Since* HE *has neglected to release the safety, his pistol refuses to fire. The* COUNT, *however, has made the necessary adjustment and, turning, fires bravely into the air and grandly falls. The* SMOKEWEAVER *rushes to* HIM *with mock solicitude. The* COUNTESS *goes to* HOLLIS *to instruct him in the operation of the gun.* IVY, *aware that all is over, fearfully opens her eyes. When* SHE *can see that the* COUNT *is the victim,* SHE *cries out to* HOLLIS *in panic and indignation.*

IVY: You brute, you've killed him!

HOLLIS, *who has finally removed the safety catch, in his surprise fires inadvertently in no special direction. The* COUNT *twitches horribly and groans)*

And super-brute for shooting him again when he is down!

HOLLIS: *(In despair)* What did she say?

The COUNTESS *comforts him.*

IVY: *(Rushing over to the* COUNT*)* Ah, my poor darling!

The COUNT *sneezes.*

Angel, you're still alive!

SHE *is down beside* HIM, *holding* HIM *in her arms.*

COUNT: *(Sepulchrally)* Only just, Ivy.

IVY: Ah, my Count, my Count, can you forgive me for the shameful way I have treated you?

COUNT: Only just, Ivy.

IVY: *(His head on her bosom)* My love, my only...

SHE *strokes* HIM, *soothingly. The* COUNT *suppresses a laugh, manages to convert it to a moan.*

Oh dear! Have I hurt you more?

COUNT: No; just tickled a bit.

IVY: I shall be your nurse now; I shall bind your wounds.

Searching for the wound.

This is strange, I...

SMOKEWEAVER: Ahem. I think you'd better leave the Count to the Countess. She's had...

Ignoring her father, IVY *continues her investigation, now somewhat frantically.*

IVY: But, Father, I don't see that the Count has been wounded at all.

As SHE *tickles* HIM.

COUNT: Hey, hey!

HE *wriggles free of* HER; *rises.*

SMOKEWEAVER: Remarkable recovery, I must say. Sturdier man than you'd think to look at him.

IVY: *(With mounting indignation)* Has this been some kind of joke? Were there real bullets in those pistols?

SMOKEWEAVER: *(Smiling sheepishly)* Well…

IVY: *(Rising in fury)* Well, I never!

The SMOKEWEAVER *and* COUNTESS *laugh outright. The* COUNT *is chucking, while* HOLLIS *is thoroughly bewildered.*

What a lot of wicked children you all are, to play upon my sympathies and make me look the fool. If this is how supposed adults take seriously honor and love and all the important things of life, I am glad I am not one minute older than I am.

HOLLIS: Ivy, I…

IVY: Don't come near me, Hollis Greengage.

HOLLIS: But, Ivy…

IVY: Don't speak to me. Don't any man speak to me. I'm through with men forever.

SHE *stamps up the steps into the house, slamming the door behind her.* HOL-LIS *looks after* HER. *A pause.* HOLLIS *turns to the* SMOKEWEAVER, *who has come up behind him.*

HOLLIS: She's very unreliable, isn't she.

SMOKEWEAVER: She is that, Hollis.

COUNT: It's rather a long time: forever.

COUNTESS: When I was a girl we reckoned it in days. Three made quite an encroachment on forever. These youngsters today have so stepped up the pace. I imagine three hours are now very close to eternity.

HOLLIS *has moved away from the others, brooding. The* SMOKEWEAVER *comes to* HIM.

SMOKEWEAVER: What's the trouble, my boy?

HOLLIS: Trouble?

SMOKEWEAVER: You look a bit down in the mouth. Aren't you relieved that nobody was hurt?

HOLLIS: Oh, yes, I'm relieved about all that, but Ivy…

SMOKEWEAVER: You should have trusted me, Hollis. I said everything would come out all right.

HOLLIS: You did indeed, sir; and I trusted you – sort of. It would have helped some if you had told me about the blanks.

COUNT: An unfortunate oversight.

COUNTESS: But it proved something, I think.

SMOKEWEAVER: I think it did. You're a fine lad, Hollis. *(More brightly)* Oh, if you could have seen your face when I handed you that pistol!

COUNTESS: Very grave.

SMOKEWEAVER: And your farewell to Ivy!

COUNT: Ever so touching.

SMOKEWEAVER: And just the slightest bit ridiculous.

HOLLIS: I guess it seemed that way to you; but, you see, I didn't know for sure…

SMOKEWEAVER: Of course, you didn't Hollis. But the point is that you should have known. Is it reasonable to think we should have let you fight a proper duel? We may behave at times like idiots, but, generally speaking, you must allow us a degree of common sense.

HOLLIS: *(Beginning to smile)* I suppose I did look pretty silly.

SMOKEWEAVER: You had nothing on the Count, my boy. He fell magnificently. Too bad you weren't looking at the time; you'd have seen quite a performance.

To the COUNT.

Would you care to repeat it now for Hollis's benefit?

COUNT: I'm not sure that I can; I haven't had sufficient preparation.

COUNTESS: Go on, you ham.

COUNT: Well…

SMOKEWEAVER *makes a pistol of his thumb and forefinger and points it at the* COUNT.

SMOKEWEAVER: BANG!

The COUNT *clutches melodramatically at his heart and begins to stagger.*

COUNTESS: He's off!

The COUNT *careens about the stage, collapsing finally into a chair. All roar with laughter, this time including* HOLLIS. *Unnoticed,* IVY *comes out of the house, keeping her distance from them.*

IVY: *(Sharply)* Hollis!

COUNT: Ohoh, eternity is up already.

COUNTESS: Even sooner than I expected.

IVY: *(Succumbing to curiosity)* What are you all doing?

SMOKEWEAVER: Aha! Miss Curiosity!

Composing herself; ignoring her father.

IVY: Hollis, I wanted to talk to you; it might be worth your while to stop laughing a moment and listen to me.

HOLLIS *tries to keep a straight face.*

HOLLIS: Of course, Ivy. What is it?

IVY: I have been giving the matter some very serious consideration.

COUNTESS: *(Apart, to* COUNT*)* For all of three minutes.

COUNT: Ssh! I think we're about to be favored with an important revelation.

HOLLIS: Yes, Ivy?

IVY: It has occurred to me that your frivolous behavior this morning seems hardly typical of the boy whom I have long regarded as nothing if not serious-minded. It may be that my father and the Count have beguiled you into joining in a prank which it would have not been like you to initiate yourself. You are still quite young, Holly, and rather innocent; and therefore there may yet be grounds to hope for your salvation. If so, I should be less than kind to abandon you to these gentlemen's corrupting influence. You asked me yesterday to be your teacher, and I declined the invitation for what seemed sufficient reason at the time. But, as long as there is no question of a romantic attachment between us, perhaps I could arrange...I wish you'd stop grinning at me; it's very disconcerting.

HOLLIS: *(Ready to burst)* I'm sorry, Ivy; it's just that you're so funny when you talk like that.

IVY: Hollis, I'm disappointed in you. I had hoped so much to save you at least; but now I see you're lost, absolutely lost. *(Turning away, suddenly, in tears)* Oh, what am I going to do?

SMOKEWEAER *puts his hands on his daughter's shoulders.*

SMOKEWEAVER: Ivy, darling... *(*SHE *shrugs him away.* HE *persists)* Now, now, now.

IVY: *(Pouting)* Yes, Father.

SMOKEWEAVER: Don't you take that tone of voice with me, young lady.

Turning HER *around.* SHE *hangs her head.*

Now, I just want to ask you a question: Why in thunder are you so concerned about saving Hollis. I seem to recall your saying you were through with men – all men – forever.

IVY: I know I said that, but I am privileged to change my mind. *(The* SMOKEWEAVER *chuckles.* SHE *goes to the* COUNTESS*)* You understand, Countess, don't you? Men are impossible creatures really, but we women of the world must learn to endure them – or else be terribly lonely.

The COUNTESS *takes the* COUNT'S *hand.*

COUNTESS: I have always clung to that opinion.

HOLLIS *laughs outright.*

IVY: *(Turning on* HIM*)* There you go again! I don't know what's got into you, Hollis Greengage: everything I say you take to be a joke. And to think I thought you loved me!

HOLLIS: *(Seriously)* I do, Ivy; more, I believe, than ever. But there's a difference now.

IVY: Oh?

HOLLIS: You see, now I love you for what you are and not for what you pretend to be.

IVY: Pretend!

HOLLIS: *(Very earnestly)* Yes, Ivy. I know that you don't think that you're pretending, but you can't always tell where the world leaves off and your dreams begin. That's really being childish, you know. When your father and the Count pretend, they're only fooling you – and sometimes me – but I don't think they often fool themselves.

IVY: *(Flabbergasted)* Hollis, how can you talk to me like that?

HOLLIS: *(Calmly)* Because I'm not afraid of you any more.

SMOKEWEAVER: *(Apart, to* COUNT *and* COUNTESS*)* Today our boy has become a man.

IVY: *(Awed)* Holly, you're so masterful! *(To* SMOKEWEAVER*)* I'm ready to marry him, Father.

SMOKEWEAVER: Whoa, whoa, whoa! Don't you think Hollis should have his say in this?

IVY: He's had his say already. He proposed to me yesterday.

SMOKEWEAVER: Is this true, Greengage? *(*HOLLIS *nods)* And are your intentions regarding my daughter still honorable?

Hollis: Very much so, sir – only…well…

SMOKEWEAVER: *(Apart, to* HOLLIS*)* Say no more, by boy! I understand perfectly.

IVY: Well, Father, do we have your permission or… *(An idea intrigues* HER*)* Must Holly and I elope?

SMOKEWEAVER: You must do nothing of the kind. As long as you are under age, Ivy, the law forbids your marrying without your parent's consent; and that, I regret to say, I must withhold. *(*IVY *starts to object)* Uh-uh, don't interrupt. You see, my dear, I must consider my own situation. Here I am utterly dependent upon you: you cook for me and darn my socks and sew the buttons on my shirts. Without you I shouldn't know how to take care of myself; so, before you go running off with a husband, you'll have to teach me at least the rudiments of housekeeping. *(To* HOLLIS, *with mock gravity)* And, alas, I'm a slow learner, Hollis.

HE *winks at* HOLLIS.

IVY: Oh, Father, how selfish of me! I never thought…

SMOKEWEAVER: *(Putting* HIS *arm about* HER; *looking very noble)* That's all right, my girl.

COUNT: *(Apart to* HOLLIS*)* Does that answer your problem, Hollis?

HOLLIS: Very well, sir.

SMOKEWEAVER: *(Beginning to "lay it on")* Besides, Ivy, though you may be of too tender years to be a wife, you're just the perfect age to be a daughter.

The COUNTESS *pantomines playing a violin and hums a bar from something like Mendelssohn's "Spring Song."*

IVY: I love you, Father.

SMOKEWEAVER: That's my girl. *(To* HOLLIS*)* You must forgive me, Hollis, if I cling to her a little while longer; but I promise you, sir, one day I shall be proud to call myself your father-in-law. Do you think you can wait till then?

HOLLIS: I shall wait.

> †*Song:* (SMOKEWEAVER, COUNT, COUNTESS)
> Then we shall celebrate the day
> When Holly bears his bride away
> With rigadoon and roundelay
> And other evidence of joy;
> All through the watches of the night
> We shall prolong the merry rite
> To do, with laughter and with light,
> Honor to our girl and boy.
>
> CHORUS:
> Sing down-down-derry and fa-la-la,
> Sing hey-diddle-diddle, sing oom-pah-pah,
> Sing hi-no-nonny, et cetera,
> For Holly and for Ivy.
>
> And then we must contrive a charm
> All evil spirits to disarm
> Lest any hate or any harm
> Between their loves should intervene;
> A magic circle we shall wind
> That will their hearts together bind,
> In one bright garland all entwined
> The Holly and the Ivy green.
>
> CHORUS:
> Sing down-down-derry and fa-la-la,
> Sing hey-diddle-diddle, sing oom-pah-pah,
> Sing hi-no-nonny, et cetera–
> The holly and the ivy.

SMOKEWEAVER: Ivy, all this cavorting around has given me an appetite. Isn't it about time you fixed some lunch?

IVY: Oh, yes, Father. *(An afterthought)* Can Holly stay?

SMOKEWEAVER: Well now, I think we've kept him from his family long enough.

HOLLIS: But I'll come by tomorrow, Ivy.

IVY: I shall expect you every day, Holly.

COUNT: *(Hesitatingly)* Ahem! I suppose I'm not exactly in your best graces, but…

IVY: *(Somewhat formally)* Oh, Count, I forgave you long ago.

COUNT: I'm glad to hear that, Ivy, for I should like to feel free to drop by now and again myself.

COUNTESS: You're not thinking of going back into the serenade business?

COUNT: *(Genuinely appalled)* Oh, Great Heavens, no! *(To* IVY*)* I mean only to play checkers with your father.

IVY: You will always be welcome, Count. Good-bye Holly.

SHE *blows* HOLLIS *a kiss and goes into the house.*

HOLLIS: *(To* SMOKEWEAVER*)* How long will it have to be, sir?

SMOKEWEAVER: You know the answer to that, Hollis: as long as it takes her to learn to laugh at herself.

The COUNT *sneezes fiercely.*

COUNTESS: Come home you aged invalid, and we'll attend to that.

COUNT: Yes, nurse. *(To* HOLLIS*)* Holly, my boy, if I survive this cold, I shall probably drink myself to death with the elixir on your wedding day.

HOLLIS: That would be very unfortunate, sir.

COUNTESS: Don't worry; I shall be there to restrain him.

COUNT: I daresay you will. Let's go.

HE *leaves, left, followed by* COUNTESS.

SMOKEWEAVER: Holly, you know, it occurs to me that if you are to be my son-in-law, you must be prepared to support my daughter in the manner to which she is used. I have always regretted since my retirement that I've left no successor to my trade. I should be very glad, if it would interest you, to teach you all the secrets of a smokeweaver. His is not a very lucrative profession; but it has its own rewards, and competitors are few, indeed too few. Above all, Ivy would be very pleased. What do you say?

HOLLIS: Oh, thank-you, sir. I'd be most happy to accept an apprenticeship.

SMOKEWEAVER: Splendid. We shall start tomorrow. Now you'd better be running home.

HOLLIS: Yes, sir, but…

SMOKEWEAVER: What is it, Holly?

HOLLIS: I'm embarrassed to say this, but I really don't know what a smokeweaver is.

SMOKEWEAVER: No need for embarrassment, my lad. As for what a smokeweaver is, that's very easily explained. A smokeweaver is a man who weaves smoke; it's as simple – and as difficult – as that. Not ordinary smoke, mind you, but smoke that he has colored cunningly by processes which you will learn in time. He weaves it, woof on warp – a most delicate operation; and when he has done so...

> He casts his web of smoke into the air;
> It hangs, a subtle fabric, trembling there
> A moment till the wind destroys it; then
> It's gone: no art can bring it back again.
> And if you ask what use it has, I'll say
> No more than wreathes of flowers have in May,
> Or stories told before a winter fire,
> Or singing birds in cages of gold wire,
> Or, in a bustling breeze, a small boy's kite,
> Or anything that serves for man's delight.

To the audience.

> Our play is done. We bid you all good-night.
>   CURTAIN

THE LAST OF THE MAMMOTHS

The Last of the Mammoths

This play has never had a staged performance, but it has been given several public readings, all of them in New York. The first was produced in 1979 by Dino Narizzano at his Soho Artists Theatre, with Joseph Warren as the "Judge." In 1994, it was read for an invited audience at Polaris North and again, in 1997, at the Episcopal Actors' Guild. This latest reading was directed by Tom Ferriter with Keith Partington as the narrator and the following cast:

"Judge" Calvin Gorse. Barnard Hughes
Emily Gorse . . . . Helen Stenborg
Patsy Connor. . . . . Laura Hughes
Neil Connor . . . . Jamie Nelson Simon
Oliver Purdy . . . . Peter Harris
Joe Hapgood . . . . Jerry McGee
Laurine Hapgood . . . . Pamela Nigro

cast of characters
(in order of appearance)

"Judge" Calvin Gorse: about seventy years old, tall, heavy-set, white-maned, full enough of years, but still full of vigor.

Emily Gorse: his wife: in her late fifties, a tall, heavy-boned, handsome woman; strong, but not unfeminine; warm, though not greatly sentimental – and fundamentally much less so than the Judge. She wears but a little make-up; and her hair has been simply, but attractively, styled; the little jewelry she wears is of good quality.

Patsy Connor: their daughter: in her late twenties, a younger and better educated version of her mother, not a "pretty-girl" type, but attractive.

Neil Connor: her husband: early thirties, good-looking, wiry build, bright.

Oliver Purdy: of an age with the Judge, but a small, thin, pinched man with strands of black hair plastered against the sallow egg-crown of his skull. To many he seems rather stand-offish and dour; but, with the Judge, he is completely at ease, an elf, a New England leprechaun.

Joe Hapgood: in his forties, not much taller than his wife, a trim, stocky man, obviously in excellent physical shape. He has a well-scrubbed look and is immaculately dressed in rather conservative summer attire. His manner is perfectly friendly, but less ebullient, more reserved than his wife's.

Laurine Hapgood: his wife: a short, plump woman, rather overdressed, with much costume jewelry and dyed blond hair; not hard, however, but very warm and bubbly, completely at ease.

act I
Scene. 1: The living-room of the Gorses' home in a rural Connecticut township; early evening of a Friday in August.
Scene. 2: The same; Saturday morning.

act II
Scene. 1: Deacon's Pond; late Saturday afternoon.
Scene. 2: The Gorses' living-room; Sunday afternoon.

time: 1962

ACT ONE
Scene One

The living-room of the Gorses' home in Sudbury, a rural Connecticut township. The room constitutes an ell of the house. Spacious and comfortable, it comprises two quite separate areas, one of which is dominated by a large fireplace, a deer head over the mantle, crammed bookshelves on either side, storage cabinets beneath the shelves. Here are also a large, well-worn, leather-covered sofa, over-stuffed easy chairs, and a cobbler's bench. The other part of the room is relatively bare. The principal piece of furniture here is a large work-table with flanking benches. There is also a dresser with drawers and a shallow cupboard with shelves above, containing plates and glasses, and a closed cabinet below, which serves as a liquor closet. Elsewhere about the room is the customary complement of lamps, tables, straight-backed chairs and a wastepaper basket. On the walls are Currier and Ives prints, old photographs (one of them with a faded Yale pennant stuck behind it) and a gun-rack supporting a brace of shotguns, a deer rifle, and several rod cases.

This is a family room, for working, for loafing, and for informal dining. The various objects – on the tables, on the shelves, on the cobbler's bench – bespeak the interests of CALVIN *and* EMILY GORSE. *His law-books and fishing tackle; her gardening encyclopedias and sewing materials. The litter is casual, "homey" – and considerable.*

A door leads to a formal parlor, carefully decorated, furnished with fine antiques and almost never used – except that the telephone is in there. Beyond the parlor would be the entrance hall and the main door of the house. There is a side entrance, leading outdoors here in the living-room. The windows here also provide access to the outside; they are wide and tall – reaching from the floor almost to the ceiling – French doors, in effect, a somewhat modern improvement in an otherwise old-fashioned room.

The windows are open. It is early evening; Friday of the first week of August.

JUDGE CALVIN GORSE *and* OLIVER PURDY *are seated across from each other at the long table. Between them is a welter of fishing paraphernalia – fly-books, leader boxes, a net, a creel containing two plump small-mouth bass in a nest of ferns. The* JUDGE *is sorting out his collection of dry flies.* OLIVER *is working through a tangle of line.*

There is a long pause as THEY *work.* OLIVER *is having trouble with his knotted line.*

OLIVER: Darn! *(After a moment)* Some kind of gremlin has been at these knots.

JUDGE: Let it go, Ollie. We've got enough line to string up every bass in Deacon's Pond from now to Doomsday.

OLIVER: *(Absorbed in his work)* I ought to be able to untie this.

JUDGE: Maybe if you said a spell over it.

OLIVER: How's that, Cal?

JUDGE: Inty minty sibbity sab, Ibbity bibbity canarbo.

OLIVER: *(Catching on)* Canarbo in, canarbo out, Canarbo up the water spout!

TOGETHER: O U T spells out goes Y O U!

THEY *laugh, shake their heads, resume work. Pause.*

JUDGE: Did it work?

OLIVER: *(Absorbed)* No.

Pause.

JUDGE: *(Holding up a fly)* I'm sorry, Ollie, but this one's no damn good. It looks like a Maybug to me; it looks like a Maybug to you; but to a hungry bass it just doesn't say a thing.

OLIVER: Burnham Coates swears by it. Won't use anything else.

JUDGE: Burnham Coates! I was casting dry flies into Deacon's Pond when he didn't know a bass from his backside.

OLIVER: *(Glumly)* Yes. I don't know why he has to horn in on our lake.

JUDGE: Just don't think about it, Ollie. Worrying won't do anybody any good.

OLIVER: Well, I worry. There must be some way out of it, Cal.

JUDGE: Have you got fifty thousand dollars?

OLIVER: If Augusta weren't ailing, I could...

JUDGE: Well, I surely couldn't. And even if we could scrape up a hundred thousand between us, if Burnie wants the place, he'll outbid any offer we make.

EMILY GORSE *has come in while her husband was speaking.* SHE *carries an ice bucket and a pitcher of water on a tray.*

EMILY: Are you still fretting about that property on Deacon's Pond?

JUDGE: Ollie's fretting.

OLIVER: Why shouldn't I be? Can you imagine what it would look like after Burnie Coates got through with it?

JUDGE: *(With exaggerated solemnity)* Gracious lawns extending from the great house to the marges of the lake.

OLIVER: A formal French garden.

JUDGE: An informal English garden full of mignonette.

HE *improvises a minuet.* EMILY *dissolves in laughter.*

OLIVER: All that – what do they call it – topiary?

JUDGE: And espalier fruit trees.

EMILY: *(Teasing)* How nice!

JUDGE: Emmy!

OLIVER: You know what I heard? He's got a whole lot of statues in a warehouse in New York; brought them over from Italy. Wood nymphs and stuff like that.

All very – you know! *(Indicating characteristically female curves)* Sorry, Emily.

EMILY: Not at all, Oliver; they sound quite delightful.

OLIVER: As a matter of fact, Cal, they probably are pretty goldurned good. Those four little Fragonard panels of Burnie's are absolutely out of this world. I'd give my eyeteeth for just one of them. If only Augusta...

JUDGE: Nobody ever said Burnham Coates didn't have good taste.

EMILY: Exquisite taste.

JUDGE: In some things.

OLIVER: It's not a question of taste, Emily; it has to do with the fitness of things. If Burnie were buying in Newport or somewhere down on Long Island, his idea of a home for himself would be just fine. But it simply doesn't go on the shore of our little Deacon's Pond.

EMILY: I know what you mean, Oliver. But I really don't think Burnham's going to buy that property after all.

JUDGE: What makes you say that?

OLIVER: They're searching the deed now.

JUDGE: And I happen to know it's as clean as a hound's tooth.

EMILY: Mildred Coates has something to say about it, and she wants to live in California.

JUDGE: You don't say!

EMILY: She said as much to Esther Bainbridge yesterday.

OLIVER: No!

EMILY: Not in so many words; but I think it makes a great deal of sense, don't you? She'd be bored to death living here, year in, year out. And Burnham, too. They've just been carried away, spending a month here roughing it.

JUDGE: Roughing it!

OLIVER: Did you hear? Burnie bought a brand-new, fancy-Dan hunting jacket from Abercrombie and Fitch. Buried it for a week behind the garage to give it that "aged" look.

JUDGE: Takes a thermos bottle of martinis in the boat with him, so as not to miss his cocktail hour.

EMILY: They've been playing games, that's all. Mildred's getting tired of it already; and Burnham's going to give up pretty soon. Just see if he doesn't.

JUDGE: Perhaps you're right, Emmy.

OLIVER: I hope so; I certainly hope so.

EMILY: Cheer up, Ollie. I'm sure I am. Everything's going to be all right.

OLIVER: Well, I don't know.

EMILY: Wait and see.

OLIVER: Can't do anything else, I guess.

JUDGE: Even if Burnham does buy the place, it could be a damnsight worse. Suppose one of those development fellows got a hold of it. How would you like to see a flock of little cabins up there, all with names like "Bide-a-Wee" and "Welcome Inn"?

OLIVER: Or "No Namie". I saw that one once.

JUDGE: *(With incredulity and disgust)* "No Namie"?

OLIVER: *(Glumly)* "No Namie."

JUDGE: Jesus!

OLIVER: I don't want to think about it.

EMILY: Don't. It's no use, Oliver. *(Noticing the creel of fish; with feigned indignation)* Phew! Those smelly things! How do you expect to eat here with those on the table?

JUDGE: Now, Emmy, don't get into a sweat: I was going to take them out into the kitchen.

OLIVER: I'll take them out.

EMILY: Oh, Oliver, you don't have to do that.

OLIVER: I have to wash my hands anyway. *(Dumping the tangled line on the table)* I can't do anything about this.

JUDGE: Let it go.

OLIVER: Well, I just thought…

JUDGE: *(Sharply; moving the tangle out of* OLIVER'S *reach)* Ollie! For Chrissakes!

OLIVER: I'll take the fish.

EMILY: Thank you, Oliver. *(*OLIVER *picks up the creel and starts for the kitchen)* Ollie, why don't you stay for supper? We're just having cold cuts and a salad in here. Nothing fancy.

OLIVER: Well, that sounds…

EMILY: We'll be eating as soon as the children arrive.

OLIVER: On second thought, I'd better get back to Augusta. It's Jenny Mae's night off, and Gussie gets kind of restless when she's left alone.

EMILY: Just as you say, Oliver.

OLIVER *goes out. The* JUDGE *begins to stow away his fishing gear, while* EMILY *sets the table.*

JUDGE: Changed his mind pretty quick about that dinner invitation, eh?

EMILY: He can't forget Augusta very long. I sometimes wonder how sick she really is. If I had to hold you so desperately, Cal, perhaps I'd be an invalid, too.

JUDGE: I hope you never have to, Emmy.

EMILY: I'll never have to. I've learned that the only way you can hold anything in this world is to be willing to let it go.

The JUDGE *has picked up the tangled fishing line.* HE *hesitates a moment, then drops it into the wastepaper basket.*

JUDGE: Say what you like about old Gussie, she's Ollie's curse, but she's also his excuse.

EMILY: How do you mean?

JUDGE: You know what really made him change his mind: you said the children were coming.

EMILY: But he adores Patsy. If she were his own daughter, he'd...

JUDGE: Not Patsy; Neil. I'm not quite sure what Neil is, but he's beyond Ollie's pale anyway. Why, Ollie won't even speak to a Democrat, not since he stopped selling insurance.

EMILY: *(Softly)* I know.

JUDGE: Heard him say a kind word about Grover Cleveland once.

A pause.

EMILY: Is Neil a Communist, Cal?

JUDGE: Hell no! He's too damn independent. Can you imagine his taking orders from a cell leader?

EMILY: I guess not.

JUDGE: More likely he'd be telling Mr. Khrushchev how *Pravda* should "liberalize its editorial policy." Something like that.

A long pause as THEY *go about their work. After a while the* JUDGE *is still puttering; but* EMILY *has stopped in her tracks and is staring off into space. Finally, the* JUDGE *notices her.*

JUDGE: *(Waving his hand in front of her eyes)* Hello, Emily Cushman Gorse. Are you still with us?

EMILY: I'm still here. I was just thinking.

JUDGE: If only Patsy had married John Bainbridge.

EMILY: Yes.

JUDGE: Well, she didn't, Emmy. She's a big girl; she made her own choice; and, in a manner of speaking, it's none of our goddam business.

EMILY: I keep telling myself that, but I'm still not quite convinced. Johnny's such a kind boy, so sweet, so gentle, so considerate; he'd have made Patsy such a lovely husband.

JUDGE: Oh, I'm not so sure. Perhaps our little Button Bright gets all the sweetness she wants right here. Neil gives her something else she needs. I don't know what exactly.

EMILY: He's so hard, Cal.

JUDGE: Well, yes.

EMILY: And Patsy's getting hard, too. That's what frightens me.

JUDGE: Getting hard! She's been a tough little customer for a long while now.

EMILY: I hate to admit it, but I think you're right. I don't know how she got that way. Not from us, Cal, surely.

JUDGE: College perhaps, that job in New York, I don't know. Maybe it's just the younger generation. Look at those Winfield kids putting that Pond property on the market, and it's been in their family over seventy-five years. These youngsters just don't seem to care any more.

EMILY: You can't say that, Cal. Bud Winfield didn't leave the boys a cent, and they all live out of the state. Why should they hang on to that place?

JUDGE: Well, they ought to, well...

HE *is not in the least bit sure what they ought to do.*

EMILY: Have we failed Patsy in some way?

JUDGE: *(Angry)* Hell, no! Stop brooding about it, Emmy, you're worse than Ollie over that damn lake. Think positively. Isn't that the lesson for the day? Neil comes from a decent family; he...

EMILY: But they're from Michigan.

JUDGE: I have some startling news for you, Emmy: some quite nice people come from Michigan.

EMILY: I guess so. *(A quiet afterthought)* Fords.

JUDGE: I was saying: his family is all right; he's got a good job; he's a brainy fellow.

EMILY: He scares me he's so smart.

JUDGE: Well, Patsy's smart, too.

EMILY: I can't seem to reach him.

JUDGE: Maybe you don't have to. That's Patsy's job.

EMILY: Oh, Cal, why do you have to take his side every time?

JUDGE: Whoah now! Whoah now!

EMILY: You're just as upset as I am. You can't get through to him, either, and it annoys the dickens out of you. I've seen it happen time and time again.

Pause.

JUDGE: *(Very softly)* You're right, Emmy dear. If misery loves company, you've got company. Now are you satisfied?

EMILY: Oh, Cal.

JUDGE: *(Putting his arm around her)* It's all right. I was just trying to...

EMILY: I know. (SHE *breaks away from him and goes to turn on a light in the darkening room. Impulsively, the* JUDGE *comes up behind her, throws his arms about her, kisses the nape of her neck.* SHE *is startled, but her indignation is feigned)* Cal! What on earth do you think you're doing?

JUDGE: Just being a dirty old man.

HE *sits.*

EMILY: I should think so! Molesting ladies!

JUDGE: *(Pulling her down beside him)* Do you very much mind my molesting you?

EMILY: Mind? I'm flattered.

JUDGE: *(His arm about her)* Emmy, Emmy, you're the only person in the world that matters to me. All the rest can go to hell; and that, I'm afraid, includes Neil Connor.

EMILY: And Patsy too?

JUDGE: *(Somewhat off-guard)* No; of course not. Button Bright means a very great deal to me.

EMILY: But?

JUDGE: *(Patting her hand; his final say on the matter)* Emily, you're my girl.

EMILY: Yes, Cal. *(She leaves him and goes to finish setting the table. Pause)* Did you have a nice time on the lake today?

JUDGE: Pretty good.

EMILY: *(Still at work)* That was a foolish question, I suppose.

JUDGE: Not at all, Emmy. Some days are better than others.

EMILY: But they're all pretty good?

JUDGE: Oh, yes; but today, as a matter of fact, was a little better than average. Besides the two we got, Ollie raised one in the north bay.

EMILY: Big one?

JUDGE: Oh, pretty fair.

HE *relaxes into a genial reverie.*

EMILY: *(After a moment)* Did it happen again?

JUDGE: *(Glowing)* Yes.

EMILY: Then it was a good day.

JUDGE: *(Softly)* It always happens.

EMILY: *(Having finished her work)* So it's always good.

JUDGE: That's right, Emmy. That's right.

EMILY *gives him an affectionate pat and starts to go out through the parlor door.* SHE *runs into* OLIVER *returning with the fishing creel, now empty, and a small packet neatly wrapped in butcher's paper.*

EMILY: Oh, Oliver!

JUDGE: That was just about the longest hand-wash I ever did see.

OLIVER: But I...

JUDGE: Oliver Purdy, I strongly suspect you snuck over to Minnie Yankovitch's and tore off a quick one.

EMILY: Cal!

OLIVER *begins to giggle, then shake with laughter.*

JUDGE: Haven't you noticed, Emmy? Whenever he gets downwind of Minnie Yank, he's hotter than a beagle on the trail of a buck rabbit. Have a care, Ollie: Steve Yankovitch has a mighty powerful set of biceps.

OLIVER: No fear of that, Cal; no fear at all. There was a time when Minnie's charms might have raised a spirit in this frail body. But that spirit has been laid forever, I'm afraid. And old Minnie's gone a bit around the bend, too, if the truth be known.

EMILY: *(Kidding)* Really! I don't think I should be listening to this.

SHE *starts again for the door.*

OLIVER: I cleaned the fish for you.

| EMILY: | JUDGE: |
| How sweet of you, Oliver! | Hell, you didn't have to do that! |

OLIVER: No trouble at all. I'm taking mine home with me, *(*HE *holds up the package)* Unless, of course, you'd like it for your breakfast, Emily.

EMILY: Not me; thank you, Oliver. Bass always makes me break out.

OLIVER: All right then. *(As* EMILY *goes out through the parlor, calling after her)* See you, Emily.

EMILY: *(Within)* Good night, Oliver.

OLIVER *looks after her, then turns to the* JUDGE *when* HE *is sure* SHE *is out of earshot.*

OLIVER: Cal, I just remembered, I've got a new one for you!

JUDGE: What's that, Ollie?

OLIVER: One for the collection, Cal.

JUDGE: Really? Well, fire away!

OLIVER: Cookie Cuthbert and her Quartet of Cuddlesome Cuties!

JUDGE: No!

OLIVER: Yes.

JUDGE: You made it up, Ollie; you made it up!

OLIVER: Now, Cal, you know I couldn't make up something like that. You might; but I couldn't in a month of Sundays.

JUDGE: Ollie, are you still an unbeliever? Is there still lurking somewhere in the secret chambers of your heart the smallest suspicion that I invented Bunny Bits, the Breakfast of the Brave?

OLIVER: Oh no, Cal; not the smallest. But you mustn't think I invented Cookie Cuthbert either. As a matter of fact, I read about her in...oh, dear!

JUDGE: *(Sternly)* Where, Oliver?

OLIVER: Something called...I think it was...

JUDGE: *(Relentless)* Yes?

OLIVER: *(Guiltily)* Passionate Detective. *(The* JUDGE *bursts out laughing)* I read it at the barber's. It was just sort of lying there, and I picked it up. Casually, you know.

JUDGE: I'm sure you did, Ollie; I'm sure you did. Very casually.

OLIVER: You don't believe me.

JUDGE: Of course, I do, Ollie.

OLIVER: I think it's almost as good as Bunny Bits, don't you?

JUDGE: Much better! Well, just as good anyway. Yes, it's one for the collection, Ollie.

OLIVER: It is, isn't it? One for the collection. Well, I must be getting along.

HE *moves toward the open window.*

JUDGE: You can find your way all right?

OLIVER: Always have. (HE *starts to go)* Oh, shall we be going out to the lake again tomorrow?

JUDGE: If you like, Ollie. I…er…thought I might take Neil along. He's always said he'd come with me some time, and now it looks like a promise.

OLIVER: Well…hmm…come to think of it, I…

JUDGE: The kids are just up for the weekend. We'll have another belt at it as soon as they go. All right?

OLIVER: Yes; Monday maybe. It was nice today, wasn't it? Even though we got only those two.

JUDGE: It was nice, Ollie.

OLIVER: Oh, Cal, if you take Neil out tomorrow…well, I really shouldn't ask…

JUDGE: Go ahead; what is it, Ollie?

OLIVER: I was going to ask you…well…were you going to take him along those reeds in the north bay?

JUDGE: That's the best spot in the pond this summer.

OLIVER: I know. That's where my big one is.

JUDGE: He's not yours till you catch him, Oliver.

OLIVER: Yes, Cal; I was being selfish, I guess.

JUDGE: I won't take him anywhere near the north bay, Ollie.

OLIVER *cannot find words for his appreciation.* HE *clasps the* JUDGE's *hand, and clasps his free hand over their grip.*

OLIVER: *(About to go)* I'd die, Cal, if anything happened to Deacon's Pond. There's nothing else in my life any more. If anything happened, I'd just die.

OLIVER *gives the* JUDGE's *hand a final squeeze; and, before the* JUDGE *can answer him,* HE *disappears into the gathering darkness outside. The* JUDGE *remains at the window, looking out. A doorbell rings inside the house.*

EMILY'S VOICE: Hello, hello, hello!

PATSY'S VOICE: We're dreadfully late. I'm sorry, Mum.

EMILY'S VOICE: That's all right, dear.

NEIL'S VOICE: How are you, Miss Emily?

EMILY'S VOICE: Just fine, Neil.

PATSY'S VOICE: And Pop?

EMILY'S VOICE: Same as ever. Come on; he's in the living room.

NEIL'S VOICE: I'm sorry. We were late getting started.

EMILY'S VOICE: That's perfectly all right, Neil. We're just having a sort of picnic in here. Time means nothing at all.

And THEY *have arrived at the door. During the foregoing, the* JUDGE *closes the windows.* HE *turns into the room, and his eyes are brimming.* HE *produces a red bandana handkerchief and vigorously blows his nose.* HE *assumes a pose: paterfamilias expecting the greeting of his children.* PATSY *comes in from the parlor, runs over to him, and throws her arms about him.*

PATSY: Pop!

JUDGE: Well, well, well! Button Bright! Welcome home, my darling, welcome home!

NEIL *comes in, immediately followed by* EMILY.

NEIL: How are you, Judge?

JUDGE: Neil, my boy, how are you?

NEIL: Just fine. You're looking pretty good yourself.

JUDGE: I'm slowing down a little, Neil; I feel pretty good, but gradually I'm sort of subsiding.

NEIL: Go on! You'll never slow down, Judge.

JUDGE: Oh, I'm not through yet, mind you. They'll have to hit me with a pretty big stick before I'll lie still.

PATSY: Oh, Pop, don't talk like that.

JUDGE: Like what, Button?

PATSY: Lying still.

JUDGE: *(Joshing)* Face the facts, Button; face the facts.

PATSY: I'd rather not.

EMILY: He's teasing you, dear.

PATSY: Well, I wish he wouldn't.

JUDGE: Come, come now. *(Changing the subject)* Neil, what do you say to a small libation? I've picked up an 1824 Madeira; it's Mrs. Gorse's favorite tipple. My wife has rather expensive tastes. She might let you share it, though. Right, Emmy?

EMILY: Of course.

NEIL: That's a bit rich for my blood, Judge. Have you got some plain old bourbon?

JUDGE: Sure have; not so plain, but pretty old. Think I'll join you. Now, let's see.

HE *goes to the liquor cabinet and opens its doors.*

EMILY: *(To* PATSY*)* You're looking sort of peaked, dear. Have you been feeling all right?

PATSY: Sure, Mum.

JUDGE: *(Coming up with a bottle)* Here we are: bourbon. And...

HE *dives down again into the cabinet.*

EMILY: I wish you could stay longer than just a weekend. The rest would do you so much good.

PATSY: I really don't need it, Mum, and...

JUDGE: *(Bringing up a second bottle)* The Madeira! How about you, Button?

PATSY: I'll have some of that.

JUDGE: *(To* EMILY*, playfully)* Emily, is our daughter old enough to quaff the waters of confusion?

EMILY: I think so, dear.

JUDGE: Right you are. *(As* HE *pours)* It just doesn't seem possible, does it? *(Handing first one, then a second glass to* NEIL*)* Neil, will you pass that to your beautiful wife. And that to her equally beautiful mother.

EMILY: Oh, Cal, this is so sudden!

JUDGE: What do you mean "sudden"? I've been dazzled by you, Emily, for thirty-five years. *(Having poured a bourbon for* NEIL*)* That's for you, my boy. Sweeten to taste. You're sure you don't want to try the 1824?

NEIL: *(Splashing water into his glass)* Later perhaps. This will do me fine for now.

JUDGE: Just as you say. *(Pouring for* HIMSELF*)* There we are. *(Raising* HIS *glass)* A toast to you, my Button, on the occasion of your visit – one of your all-too-rare visits, I might observe – to the ancestral manse. And to you, too, Neil.

ALL *drink.*

EMILY: I was just saying to Patsy, I wish she could stay a week.

PATSY: A week!

JUDGE: Why not, Pat? The city's no place to be in the summer.

PATSY: I've so much to do. At least till we've settled the apartment.

EMILY: That's right, of course. I meant to ask you the first thing.

JUDGE: What's this? What's this? Have you moved?

EMILY: I told you, Cal.

JUDGE: *(A little peevishly)* Well, I forgot. *(Expansive again)* But sit ye down and tell us all about it.

PATSY *and* EMILY *sit.*

NEIL: At the moment, it's chaos.

PATSY: But it's going to be lovely.

EMILY: Really, dear?

PATSY: *(Warming)* And, Mum, you should see what Neil is doing. There wasn't half enough closet space...

JUDGE: Never is in houses these days. I think it's part of a national scheme to discourage saving.

PATSY: *(With an "oh-get-on-with-you" gesture)* Oh, Pop!

EMILY: And what has Neil done, dear?

PATSY: He's building a sort of cabinet unit that will take up one whole wall of the bedroom – all kinds of drawers and cubbyholes – even a dressing table, if you please. It's very ingenious.

NEIL: We've been breathing sawdust for two weeks now.

JUDGE: Well, you've come to the right place then. Nothing like Sudbury air to clear the lungs, eh, Button?

PATSY: That's right, Pop.

EMILY: I didn't realize you had such talents, Neil.

PATSY: I married a very versatile man.

JUDGE: Say, I want to give you kids something for that apartment. Remember the secretary desk we had in the parlor, Button, before I bought the one that's in there now?

PATSY: Of course; I grew up with it.

JUDGE: Exactly. *(To* NEIL, *who is signaling with his empty glass)* Help yourself, my boy. *(*NEIL *does so)* We've got it stored over the garage. I was planning to sell it, but, as Patsy says, she grew up with it, and I sort of think it ought to stay in the family. So it's yours. I might even be persuaded to pay the freight.

NEIL: Now really, Judge, we...

PATSY: That's terribly sweet of you, Pop, but...

JUDGE: It's maple, Neil, not a museum piece like the cherry that replaces it, but handsome just the same. Dates back to the Revolution, it does. *(Jesting, but there is an edge to the jest)* You could write your inflammatory articles on it and feel right at home.

PATSY: Pop, we appreciate the thought very much...

JUDGE: *(Somewhat petulantly)* Of course, if you don't want it...

PATSY: It's not that, Pop; it's just that...well, it wouldn't quite fit in with...

JUDGE: *(Downcast)* Say no more. I just thought you could use it; that's all.

NEIL: *(An edge to his jest, too)* I should remind you, Judge, our magazine is called the *New Era*; and in the new era, the revolutionary material is Formica, not maple. Besides, when I write those "inflammatory articles," I like to have plenty of space to spread out on.

JUDGE: I see.

PATSY: The fact is, Pop, we've got a desk – a sort of work table really. It's miles long, stain-proof, burn-proof, very smart looking, very modern. I like it; it's easy to dust.

JUDGE: *(Sourly)* Modern, eh?

EMILY: It makes sense, Cal. Neither of us use the secretary in the parlor. This is what we use – this table here. As Neil says, there's space to spread out.

JUDGE: Well, perhaps you're right, Emmy.

EMILY: Modern furniture is quite appropriate for a New York apartment, I think. Not too modern, of course – not what I call "modernistic."

JUDGE: All those Rube Goldberg chairs. Look as if steam-fitters built them, not cabinet makers.

PATSY: Don't worry, Pop: we haven't gone "modernistic."

NEIL: Just practical.

HE *goes up to the window to stare moodily out, sulking and nursing his drink.*

EMILY: *(Lamely)* Yes. *(An embarrassed pause)* Well, we can't keep these hungry men of ours waiting any longer. Will you give me a hand in the kitchen, Patsy dear?

PATSY: Yes, Mum. (SHE *does not go, however)* Pop, about the desk, I don't want you to think that...

JUDGE: I don't think a thing, Button – only that it's great to have you home again.

PATSY: *(Giving* HIM *a peck on the cheek)* Thanks, Pop.

SHE *starts to go.*

JUDGE: *(Expansively)* Your room's just the same as ever. We haven't changed a thing.

NEIL *winces. The* JUDGE *is quite unaware of this reaction; but* PATSY *notices – and* EMILY, *too.*

PATSY: *(After a moment)* Thanks, Pop.

SHE *goes out, passing* EMILY *at the doorway.*

EMILY: *(Sotto voce to the* JUDGE, *pointing covertly towards* NEIL) Take it easy, dear.

JUDGE: Hmm? *(But* SHE *has gone.* HE *moves toward* NEIL, *tentatively, clearing his throat)* Well...eh...

NEIL *finishes his drink, sets down the glass, starts to go.*

NEIL: I left our bags in the hall. I guess I should hustle them upstairs.

JUDGE: Oh, let them go till later, Neil. Sit yourself down, make yourself at home – unless you've got to wash your hands or something.

NEIL: We had to stop for gas the other side of town. I took care of everything then.

JUDGE: *(Gesturing an invitation to be seated)* Well?

NEIL: *(Holding up* HIS *glass)* May I have another?

JUDGE: You don't want to spoil your appetite, Neil. We'll be having supper in a few minutes.

NEIL: *(Setting down the glass)* Just as you say then.

JUDGE: No, no, no; go right ahead. This is Liberty Hall.

NEIL: *(Sitting)* It's all right. I don't need it.

There is an embarrassed pause. The JUDGE *clears his throat.*

JUDGE: I suppose it's sort of dull times around the *New Era* office these days.

NEIL: Why do you say that?

JUDGE: Well, your boy is in now; you have nothing to beef about. I thought you fellows were happy only when you were cutting into somebody.

NEIL: *(Laughing)* That's the way it is; but even "our boy" needs a little jab now and again.

JUDGE: What are you pushing this time? Free medical care? Cut-rate housing? Milk for the Hottentots?

NEIL: *(Amiably)* Oh, all of those things.

JUDGE: Just what I figured: more bread and circuses.

NEIL: No; just more bread.

JUDGE: Ah, yes: welfare, and then more welfare. Where does it end, Neil? When the government starts breathing for us?

NEIL: *(Amiably still)* I can't see you complaining about welfare, Judge. You fare pretty well yourself – 1824 Madeira and all. Don't you think others are entitled to a few creature comforts?

JUDGE: Certainly. If they earn them.

NEIL: *(Blurting it out)* Oh, now really!

JUDGE: What do you mean "really"?

NEIL: Well, you… *(Thinking better of it)* No; I'd have to have a few more drinks before I could…

JUDGE: Go ahead. Say what you're thinking. I'm not delicate.

NEIL: *(Taking a deep breath)* Well, I was going to say that you're hardly the one to talk about earning anything, are you, Judge? What I mean is: what does being a judge amount to in this neck of the woods?

JUDGE: Justice of the peace, to be exact. Amounts to damn little, Neil, in this town. Pays damn little, too.

NEIL: *(With a sweeping gesture)* It certainly doesn't pay for all this.

JUDGE: It certainly doesn't, Neil.

NEIL: Of course, you had a law practice once.

JUDGE: In a half-ass sort of way. You're quite right, my boy, I've never really worked for a living. Not what you'd call work, anyway. *(HE begins to pace; a pause, as HE collects his thoughts)* My grandfather worked. This was a going farm in his day. He'd get up at five o'clock in the morning and go right through to ten at night. Seven days a week. No paid vacations. No time-and-a-half for overtime. Kept that up till he was sixty. The only reason he slowed down then was my father made him take it easy. Pa was doing pretty well in the law by that time, and he figured the family's…er…welfare, if you like, was his responsibility. He managed to work himself to death at the ripe old age of forty-five; but he left me and my sister and Grandpa pretty nicely fixed. The point is, Neil, both my father and grandfather would have said just what I have said. And maybe they'd have had a better right.

NEIL: *(With admiration – and irony)* Judge, you sure can sweet-talk your way out of anything.

JUDGE: *(Barely restraining his temper)* Now, don't give me any of your lip, boy.

NEIL: *(Exploding)* What the hell, I… I… *(Contritely)* I'm sorry.

JUDGE: *(Now in full control; magnanimously)* That's quite all right. I started it.

NEIL: I won't disparage your father or your grandfather…

JUDGE: I thank you, Neil,

NEIL: *(The JUDGE is beginning to get his goat)* I'm sure they worked very hard. And you…well, you've kept busy, anyway.

JUDGE: *(Rather smugly)* Twenty-four hours isn't long enough for my day.

NEIL: But let's face it: they – and you – had a few breaks.

JUDGE: A few.

NEIL: But suppose your grandfather had been an invalid; suppose he hadn't inherited this land from his father; suppose your father had been an alcoholic, let's say, instead of a legal genius or whatever he was.

JUDGE: I'd have had to work then.

NEIL: Now, wait a minute, Judge…

JUDGE: *(Impatiently)* I don't have to wait, Neil; I see exactly what you're driving at. Let me tell you something – something I don't usually go around broadcasting.

NEIL: What's that?

JUDGE: I guess there must be in this township at least a dozen families that, from time to time over the years, have come to me for help – substantial help – and got it. A mother that needed an operation; a father out of work; a daughter knocked up by one of the local Romeos; a son with the brains but not the cash to go to college: they've all been able to rely on me. The Yankovitches next door – we've been supporting them now for two generations. Minnie Yank gets a helluva lot more out of Mrs. Gorse than she ever earns in our kitchen; and the same goes for Steve and the errands he runs for me now and again. What's more: they get bigger and better benefits, no questions asked, and a damnsight less red tape than they'd ever be getting from the United States government.

NEIL: But...

JUDGE: I know what you're going to say: these people are fortunate because... now, I don't want to sound smug, but... well, they happen to be my friends. But there are Calvin Gorses in every community, men, I mean, who realize that wealth confers a responsibility, who believe that, if you happen to be lucky, it's your job to spread your luck around a little. There'd be a lot more such men if the government encouraged them instead of...

NEIL: *(With a wry smile)* Taxing them so much?

JUDGE: Yes; partly that.

NEIL: Judge, do you know what you've been talking about? Why, it's nothing more than charity!

JUDGE: *(Sputtering)* Nothing more! *(Exploding)* Goddammit, of course it's charity! And what, pray tell me, is wrong with charity? Seems to me St. Paul and a few other pretty respectable parties have mentioned it rather favorably.

NEIL: But, if...

JUDGE: No, no "buts" Neil. If you're going to take that sort of line, there's no point in arguing with you.

NEIL: All right then.

The JUDGE *is restless.* HE *goes to the parlor door, but decides* HE *cannot escape that way.* HE *turns away, takes out a pair of spectacles, and begins aimlessly to polish them with his bandana.*

JUDGE: *(Muttering to* HIMSELF*)* Damn.

NEIL *is amused, but also disconcerted.* HE *crosses to the cabinet and begins to fix himself another drink. The* JUDGE *startles him by speaking, suddenly and quite cheerfully.*

JUDGE: Do you like fish, Neil?

NEIL: *(Almost spilling his drink)* How's that?

JUDGE: I was saying there's a nice bass in the ice-box for tomorrow's breakfast. Just the right size. I thought you might...

NEIL: *(Pleasantly)* Judge, as I believe you are sometimes painfully aware, I was brought up a mackerel snapper; but, since I left home and the bosom of the church, I haven't been able to look a fish in the face. Thanks just the same, though.

JUDGE: That's all right; I'll eat him myself.

NEIL: You're welcome to him.

JUDGE: You're not averse to catching them, however?

NEIL: Well I haven't...

JUDGE: I mean you're still game for a spin on the lake with me, tomorrow, aren't you?

NEIL: *(Diffidently)* Oh, sure. *(The* JUDGE, *disappointed, turns away and again there is an uncomfortable pause, till* NEIL *suddenly snaps his fingers)* Say, I just remembered. Did you see the latest issue of the *Sudbury Bulletin*?

JUDGE: No; we'll be getting our copy in the village tomorrow morning.

NEIL: Pat picked up one at the service station. There's an article in it about that lake of yours.

JUDGE: *(Brightening)* You don't say?

NEIL: I haven't read it myself; but we've got the paper out in the hall.

JUDGE: Oh, would you get it, Neil? I'd be very much interested.

NEIL: Pat thought you would be.

HE *goes out.* PATSY *and* EMILY *are heard approaching, laughing.*

EMILY'S VOICE: I wasn't aware of it at all until your father told me after we got home... Where are you going, Neil? Supper's all ready.

NEIL'S VOICE: I'll be right with you.

PATSY'S VOICE: Come on, Neil.

EMILY *enters with a platter of cold cuts and a salad bowl.*

EMILY: Food at last!

NEIL'S VOICE: *(Far off)* I'm just going to get something.

EMILY: What's the matter, Cal?

PATSY'S VOICE: Please, Neil.

JUDGE: I just can't get through to him, Emmy; I... *(*EMILY *shakes her head sympathetically.* PATSY *enters with a pitcher of iced tea. Brightly)* Well, well, well: Mother's little helper!

PATSY: *(Embarrassed)* Oh, come off it, Pop. *(As* SHE *sets the pitcher on the table)* What's my husband run off for? He's been talking about how hungry he was ever since Stamford.

JUDGE: He'll be right back. He's just getting me his copy of the *Bulletin*.

PATSY: *(To* HERSELF*)* Oh, no.

SHE *turns toward the door, unnoticed by* EMILY *and the* JUDGE.

EMILY: *(Fussing at the table)* Your father's the same way: put supper on the table, and that is just when he has to make a telephone call or...

JUDGE: *(Examining the cold cuts)* Not tonight, Emmy. Looks like you've outdone yourself this time.

EMILY: Nonsense! It's right off Mr. Harrigan's counter.

JUDGE: Well, you've done something to it.

HE *pops a piece into* HIS *mouth.* EMILY *gently slaps* HIS *hand.*

EMILY: Cal! At least sit down before you start gobbling.

JUDGE: Right you are, my dear. Patsy, come over here and sit down so your old father can nourish himself in the civilized manner to which your young mother would like to be accustomed.

EMILY: Good heavens!

PATSY: *(Pulling* HERSELF *together)* Yes, Pop.

JUDGE: The chair of honor for our favorite daughter!

HE *sits at the head of the table after* PATSY *has taken the seat indicated on his right and* EMILY *sits at the foot. The* JUDGE *begins to fork meat onto* PATSY'S *plate.*

JUDGE: How about a little ham for a starter?

PATSY: Good Lord, Pop; that's enough to feed a regiment.

JUDGE: Well, we've got to fatten you up a bit. How about you, Emmy?

EMILY: Now, don't get carried away, dear. I don't need any fattening.

JUDGE: *(Forking ham onto* EMILY'S *plate)* How's that?

EMILY: Fine, dear.

As salad is passed around:

JUDGE: Well, I must say this is nice. The whole little family together again.

NEIL *enters, newspaper in hand.* HE *might speak, but* HE *is prevented by the picture of the family group at the table, thoroughly absorbed and quite oblivious to him.* HE *clears his throat instead.* THEY *look up.*

JUDGE: Come in, my boy, come in; join the clan!

NEIL: *(With the faintest irony)* May I?

PATSY: Don't be silly, Neil.   JUDGE: Of course, of course.

EMILY: *(Indicating the seat at her right)* You just sit there, Neil, and don't let them tease you. We had to start without you because the Judge was misbehaving.

NEIL: *(Crossing and taking* HIS *seat)* I'm glad you did. I'm sorry I took so long.

JUDGE: Quite all right, my boy. Some ham?

NEIL: Thanks. *(The* JUDGE *serves* HIM. NEIL *puts the paper beside the* JUDGE'S *plate)* I had to dig around for it.

JUDGE: Oh yes; I want to see that.

PATSY: Neil, Pop doesn't want to read that now.

JUDGE: What do you mean I don't?

NEIL: He said he was interested.

PATSY: But...

JUDGE: *(Taking out* HIS *spectacles)* Of course, I am. Always interested in anything about the lake. *(*HIS *voice trails off;* HE *has begun to read.* HE *is* *evidently stunned)* Oh, no. *(He reads further)* Oh, no! I want to check up on this.

He *rises abruptly and goes out the parlor door.* EMILY *rises and follows* HIM.

EMILY: What is it Cal?

SHE *goes out. Within, the* JUDGE *is heard dialing the telephone.*

JUDGE'S VOICE: Hello… Mrs. Foster, this is Calvin Gorse, is Ray there?… Sure, I'll hang on.

PATSY: Darling, why did you do it?

NEIL: Do what? I don't see what all the fuss is about.

PATSY: Didn't you read that article?

NEIL: No; you did, and you said it was something that would interest the old man.

PATSY: I didn't say "interest," I said "horrify."

NEIL: *(Shrugging)* Apparently so.

JUDGE'S VOICE: Oh, Ray?… Cal Gorse… Fine, thank you. See here, I've just read…

EMILY *returns, closing the door after her. The* JUDGE *can no longer be heard.*

EMILY: He's calling the real estate agent. What's it all about, Patsy?

PATSY: The Winfield property's been sold.

EMILY: Oh, dear.

PATSY: *(Flaring up)* Really, Neil, I could shoot you for showing Pop that paper.

EMILY: Now, now, dear; I'm sure Neil didn't mean any harm. Your father'd have had to find out sooner or later.

NEIL: Of course, he would.

EMILY: *(To* NEIL*)* But I'm not sure you picked the best possible moment to tell him.

NEIL: *(Sincerely)* I'm sorry, Miss Emily. I guess I goofed.

EMILY: *(Somewhat coldly)* Well, there's nothing can be done about it now.

NEIL: I still don't see why there should be such a fuss about…

The JUDGE *enters, looking as if* HE *had been pole-axed.*

JUDGE: It's true.

EMILY: *(Going to* HIM*)* Patsy told me, dear. But don't worry. I promise you: I know Burnham Coates. That property will be back on the market again in less than six months. Just you wait and see. And perhaps you can do something about it then. *(He has begun to laugh, somewhat hysterically)* Why, what are you laughing about?

JUDGE: Burnham Coates! Oh, if only it could have been Burnie – with all his lawns and topiary and nymphs and satyrs and espalier fruit trees! No, my dear, Burnie Coates pulled out, just as you said he would. *(Referring to the paper)* The Winfield property has been bought by one Joseph Hapgood of Happylands Amusement Parks. So there'll be motor boats and beach cabanas, hot-dog stands, roller skating rinks, Ferris wheels, merry-go-rounds, side shows, Cookie Cuthbert and her Quartet of Cuddlesome Cuties–

Before HE can finish the catalogue, realizing HE can no longer control himself, the JUDGE flings open the door leading outside and rushes out into the night.

PATSY: *(Rising)* Pop!

SHE starts to go after him, but EMILY prevents her.

EMILY: Let him go, dear. He'll be all right in a moment. He gets so embarrassed whenever this happens.

PATSY: I've never seen Pop like that before.

EMILY: It doesn't happen very often. Perhaps not often enough. *(A pause)* He'll probably want to go over and tell Oliver Purdy.

SHE waits a moment, then goes out after the JUDGE.

NEIL: Well, the old order changeth.

PATSY: Don't, Neil.

NEIL: And it's about time.

PATSY: *(Furious)* Damn you, Neil!

SHE runs off after her father. NEIL follows her to the door, now quite concerned.

NEIL: Pat! Pat!

No answer. HE turns to go back to the supper table, notices the bourbon bottle on the cabinet, takes it to the table, sits, and is pouring HIMSELF a drink as the

CURTAIN FALLS

Scene Two

The GORSE *living room. The following morning.* EMILY *has been at work tidying the room, and the disorder of the new day's activities has not yet begun appreciably to show. The trestle table has been cleared; the magazines on the cobbler's bench have been neatly stacked; books that were left about have been returned to their shelves; ashtrays have been emptied. The windows are fully opened.* PATSY *is seated at the table, her back to the parlor door;* SHE *is lost in thought as* SHE *smokes a cigarette and sips occasionally from a coffee cup before her. Presently* NEIL *appears, bleary-eyed, at the parlor door.* SHE *is aware of his presence, but does not turn around.*

PATSY: *(Coldly)* Feeling better?

NEIL: Yes. *(A pause.* HE *comes into the room, looks for matches to light a cigarette)* Thanks for the coffee; you saved my life.

PATSY: Did you bring the cup down?

NEIL: It's in the kitchen. Washed.

PATSY: Thank you.

NEIL: *(After a moment)* Pat.

PATSY: Hmm?

NEIL: I said I was sorry.

PATSY: Fifty times.

NEIL: Well?

PATSY: And you got fried, too.

NEIL: Perhaps I wouldn't have if you had listened to me the first time.

PATSY: *(Turning towards him)* So you've got a hangover, and I'm to blame?

NEIL: Partly.

PATSY: Oh, Neil.

SHE *starts for the door with her coffee cup.* NEIL *stops her.*

NEIL: *(Suddenly forcefully)* Now, just a minute, Pat.

PATSY: What do you want?

NEIL: I want to talk to you.

PATSY: Seems to me you haven't stopped talking since last evening.

NEIL: But you haven't done anything but grunt.

PATSY: I don't know what you expect me to say.

NEIL: *(Yelling)* Well I apologized.

PATSY: *(Yelling back)* So? I heard you.

Again SHE *starts to go.*

NEIL: Wait a minute, wait a minute. *(Taking a deep breath)* I'm sorry I got drunk, too.

PATSY: *(Collecting* HERSELF; *then spelling it out to* HIM*)* Neil Connor, I don't give a damn if you got drunk. I know you hadn't read that article in the *Bulletin*, and I don't blame you for showing it to Pop. He'd have found out about the lake anyway.

NEIL: *(Bitterly)* As your mother so tactfully pointed out.

PATSY: Now, let's leave Mum out of this. She can take care of herself.

NEIL: But your old man can't, I suppose?

PATSY: No; in a way he can't.

NEIL: *(Turning away in disgust)* Oh!

PATSY: I thought you wanted me to talk.

NEIL: *(Not turning around)* Go ahead: talk.

PATSY: Oh, Neil, the hell with you!

> SHE *turns again to go and this time actually gets through the door.* NEIL *turns sharply, calling to her in panic.*

NEIL: Pat! Pat!

> SHE *gives* HIM *an anxious moment of waiting, and then returns.* PATSY *has won as many points this round as* SHE *feels* SHE *can afford in the battle between them that neither wants completely to win.* NEIL *is contrite and sincere.*

NEIL: If it's that crack I made about your father last night... *(Unable to resist the "dig," despite his contrition)* which he never even heard...

PATSY: *(Tensing)* Luckily.

NEIL: *(Humbly)* I didn't mean that.

PATSY: What? The crack last night, or...?

NEIL: *(Squirming)* Yes... I mean no...oh, Pat, I don't know.

> HE *turns away, wretchedly.* PATSY *is at ease and in control.*

PATSY: *(Gently)* I'm afraid you've meant everything right along, Neil.

NEIL: *(Bridling)* What? Now, look here...

PATSY: *(Calmly)* Let me finish. *(*HE *sulks;* SHE *goes on)* What you've said or done since we got here really doesn't matter at all; the situation in this household hasn't been affected in the least. I mean Pop would have read the paper by now anyway, and he and Mum would be doing whatever they're doing this morning whether we'd come up or not.

NEIL: Only you wouldn't have turned on the deep freeze.

PATSY: No. But – don't you see? – your actions and your words I can forgive and forget; in themselves they don't particularly count.

NEIL: Well then?

PATSY: It's your attitude, my dear.

NEIL: *(Sulkily)* About Mumsy and Popsy.

PATSY: Mostly about "Popsy."

NEIL: *(Flaring up)* Christ on a crutch! What do you expect me to do? I try. I just wish you could have heard us last night trying to have a decent conversation. Every word we said, we stepped all over each other's toes.

PATSY: I'm sure you did; but, Neil, if you'd only learn to give a little...

NEIL: *(At the top of* HIS *voice)* Give a little? Give! That man has been given to and given in to ever since the day he was born. Why, if my father had been given just one half of...

PATSY: *(Very gently)* He wasn't, Neil. It's a shame, but that's the way life goes. And don't blame Pop. He feels so guilty about his good luck. That's why he's always doing favors, even for people who don't want them. Pop has his problems, too, you see.

NEIL: I wouldn't mind a few of his problems.

PATSY: That's what it all really comes down to, isn't it, Neil?

NEIL: What?

PATSY: Envy.

HE *turns away to think a moment. When* HE *speaks again,* HE *is quite straightforward and sincere.*

NEIL: Something like that, Pat, but not quite the same. I'm jealous.

PATSY: Of me?

NEIL: *(Gently)* Who else?

PATSY: Well, I love my father, but...

NEIL: *(Suddenly bitter again)* I'll say you love your father.

PATSY: *(Shaken)* What do you mean by that?

NEIL: By what?

PATSY: *(Apprehensively)* You know perfectly well: your tone of voice, what did it mean?

NEIL: *(Brusquely trying to dismiss the matter)* My tone of voice! Look, every time I say something, you...

PATSY: What did it mean?

NEIL: *(Blasting)* How the hell... *(Muttering, as* HE *turns away)* Ask Dr. Freud or something.

There is no response from HER. HE *turns back.* PATSY *is rooted to the spot, stunned as if* HE *had hit her in the face. This time* NEIL *has won more than* HE *wanted to;* HE *goes to her with genuine solicitude and concern.*

NEIL: Pat darling, forgive me.

HE *puts his arms around her.* SHE *is submissive, rather than responsive.*

PATSY: *(In a small voice)* I love you, Neil.

NEIL: I know that. If you didn't you'd be throwing everything in the room at me now. I'm sorry, baby.

SHE *lets him kiss her on the cheek.*

PATSY: But it's perfectly normal, isn't it?

NEIL: Sure.

HE *attempts to kiss her again, but* SHE *turns her head, awkwardly bumping his mouth.* HE *instinctively puts his hand to his lips, releasing his hold upon her.*

PATSY: I mean children are supposed to love their parents, aren't they? Why does everybody have to make something sick about it?

NEIL: Everybody doesn't. Pat, I'm the one who's sick. I'm jealous. And I'm not blaming anybody else; it's all my fault. I shouldn't be jealous; I don't want to be, but...

SHE *turns toward* HIM *and smiles, almost seductively.*

PATSY: Well?

NEIL: *(Earnestly)* I need your help.

SHE *looks at* HIM *a moment; then turns away, again self-absorbed.*

PATSY: I'm scared, Neil.

NEIL: Pat.

HE *attempts to embrace her;* SHE *steps aside.*

PATSY: *(Quietly but firmly)* No.

NEIL: *(Frantically)* For God's sake, Pat, tell me please what it is you want!

SHE *turns toward* HIM. *A pause.*

PATSY: I don't want to have to choose.

NEIL *wheels away, flinging up his arms in despair. Then* HE *collects himself and tries a new tack.*

NEIL: You'll find it very hard to believe this but I really like your old man.

PATSY: *(Skeptically)* Hmm.

NEIL: I mean really. He reminds me of my own father. In certain ways.

PATSY: Does he, Neil?

NEIL: Oh, yes.

PATSY: Well, that's good for a start, isn't it?

NEIL: *(Moving towards her)* He's a charming and picturesque old gentleman. The only thing...

HE *slides an arm around* HER *shoulder.*

PATSY: *(Suspiciously)* Yes?

NEIL: Well, his view of life sort of went out with the woolly mammoth.

PATSY: *(Breaking away, disappointed)* Neil... *(Deciding on second thought to play along with him, but, nonetheless, keeping her distance)* I suppose he is rather like a mammoth, come to think of it. Big and strong, willful, blundering, magnificent.

NEIL: And extinct.

PATSY: *(Sharply)* Pop will never be extinct.

NEIL: *(Closing in on her)* Not with little Miss Mammoth to carry on the line.

PATSY: *(Stiffening)* I wasn't thinking that.

NEIL: *(Putting his arms about her)* As far as you're concerned, he's got the right answer, hasn't he?

PATSY: Yes, the right answer, Neil. *(Then yielding a little)* If not the whole answer.

HE *takes advantage of* HER *relaxation and begins to nuzzle* HER *neck.*

NEIL: Oh, baby.

PATSY: *(Pushing him away)* Stop it, Neil.

NEIL: Now what's the matter?

PATSY: I don't like to be called "baby".

NEIL: Or Button Bright?

SHE *strikes at him, a half hearted blow.* HE *seizes her arm before* SHE *can land it.*

PATSY: Let me go, Neil.

NEIL: *(Hanging onto her arm)* Come on Pat; unfreeze.

PATSY: *(Frightened)* I can't, Neil; I can't.

NEIL: Sure you can. You know damn well you can.

PATSY: Not now, Neil. Please.

NEIL: Come on.

PATSY: Please! *(There is a sound of someone in the parlor. Whispering)* Stop, Neil. Somebody's coming.

NEIL: Oh, the hell with it!

HE *releases her and would make his escape through the window, but* EMILY *prevents him, entering from the parlor with a vase of red and yellow cockscombs.* PATSY *and* NEIL *hastily compose themselves, keeping their distance from each other.*

EMILY: *(Cheerily)* Well, well, well, sleepy-heads! How are you this fine, bright morning?

NEIL: *(Glumly)* Oh, fine and bright.

HE *is near the cupboard considering the advisability of pouring* HIMSELF *a drink.*

PATSY: 'Morning, Mum.

EMILY: *(As* PATSY *kisses* HER *cheek)* Dear.

PATSY: Actually, we've been awake for hours.

NEIL: *(Looking for ice;* HIS *back to* THEM*)* You and the Judge must get up with the birds.

PATSY: *(Noticing what* NEIL *is up to; sotto voce, reproving)* There's no ice.

NEIL *looks at her, defiant, as* HE *pours himself a splash of bourbon straight.* EMILY, *setting the vase on the dresser, is unaware of this byplay.*

EMILY: Oh, before then. Often. *(To* PATSY*)* I'm sorry to be out so long. Your father wanted to go with me into the village, and...well, you know what it's like when he goes shopping.

PATSY: Say no more.

EMILY: I'll bet we stopped to talk to fifty different people.

NEIL: I didn't know there were fifty people in Sudbury.

EMILY: Saturday morning, Neil: big day in the metropolis! Everybody's in town getting groceries for Sunday dinner. Harrigants was like Macy's. *(To* PATSY, *more sentimentally)* Actually, it's fun to go with your father. Everyone is so glad to see him; everybody loves him so. But it does take time.

SHE *sits on the bench by the long table, with a little sigh. It has been a busy morning.*

PATSY: Where is Pop?

EMILY: I left him down there. He had some business with the Town Clerk, and Minnie Yankovitch gave me a lift home. *(Indicating the flowers)* Those are from her garden. Nice aren't they? A bit "kitchen-y" perhaps...but it was very sweet of her. Besides, she's helping with the dinner tonight, and she'd be disappointed if I didn't have them out.

PATSY: Are we having guests?

EMILY: Just the Lorings for bridge. You and Neil can cut in, if you like.

PATSY: You know we don't play, Mum.

EMILY: Well, we won't be at it long. They're very nice; summer people, you know. Hand me the cigarettes, dear.

PATSY *gets a box from the cobbler's bench and brings it to* EMILY, *who takes a cigarette.* PATSY *puts the box on the dresser, where* SHE *finds an ashtray and matches. Meanwhile:*

NEIL: How about a sherry, Miss Emily?

EMILY: *(Shocked)* Drinking in the morning, Neil. *(Noticing* HIS *drink; tempering* HER *remark)* No, I'm afraid I'm not that...er...progressive. I may come to it some time. Any day now!

PATSY *lights* HER *cigarette and leaves the ashtray beside* HER.

NEIL: Just as you say.

HE *finishes his drink and saunters out through the window. During the following,* HE *is seen packing back and forth, outside out of earshot.*

EMILY: *(Blowing out great clouds of uninhaled smoke)* Well, now, tell me what you've been doing this morning,

PATSY: *(Evasively)* Oh, nothing. We got up...and had breakfast...

EMILY: You didn't eat the eggs, I noticed.

PATSY: What eggs?

EMILY: I left them out for you in a bowl on the kitchen table and a frying pan all ready on the stove. All you had to do was...

PATSY: I'm sorry, Mum, but all we wanted was coffee.

EMILY: Really, dear, you ought to eat a decent breakfast. Young people especially. Any doctor will tell you that.

PATSY: Well, perhaps Neil and I aren't all that young any more. We seem to thrive on quite indecent breakfasts.

EMILY: Very well, dear. I didn't mean to be "motherly."

PATSY: *(More warmly)* We appreciated your leaving out the eggs, Mum. We just weren't frightfully hungry, that's all.

EMILY: All right. Then what did you do?

PATSY: Just came in here and talked and... *(Beginning to lose* HER *already precarious composure)* and then you came in.

EMILY: *(Noticing* PATSY'S *uneasiness; concerned)* Patsy?

NEIL *enters through the window and diverts* EMILY'S *attention.*

PATSY: *(Anxious to change the subject)* How is Pop this morning?

EMILY: Oh, he's fine.

NEIL: I thought that lake business sort of knocked him out last night.

EMILY: Down perhaps, Neil, but never out. He's got a plan now. I don't know what it is exactly; the Town Clerk has something to do with it.

NEIL: What sort of plan?

EMILY: *(Sharply)* I told you I don't know. *(More gently; to* PATSY*)* But he's fine, Patsy.

PATSY: Really?

EMILY: On the outside, yes. Oliver Purdy rather came apart last night when he heard the news. I rather think it helped your father being with him: somebody had to be the calm one. But inside, I'm sure he's got the jitters. *(To* NEIL*)* Neil, I do hope you're planning to go out on the lake with him this evening.

NEIL: Well, as a matter of fact, I...

EMILY: Please, Neil; go with him. It may not be the greatest fun in the world for you – frankly, I find it a little boring; but I'm only allowed to row the boat. But it's for men, and you're a man, and for an evening, now and again, it can be very pleasant. "A blameless pastime" – that's what he calls it. He's been so looking forward to taking you and was so disappointed when you couldn't make it last time. Don't let him down again, Neil. Especially today.

NEIL: Well...

EMILY: You understand, Neil: he's always wanted a son. *(Briskly rising)* Now I've got to start fixing some lunch.

PATSY: I'll join you in a minute, Mum.

EMILY: Take your time, dear.

SHE *goes.*

PATSY: Well?

NEIL: Well what?

PATSY: You will go out on the lake with Pop, won't you?

NEIL: I don't know.

PATSY: Oh, Neil.

NEIL: *(Feigning diffidence)* I thought it might be an idea if I got a 'phone call, say, from the magazine and had to go back to town this afternoon.

PATSY: What for?

NEIL: Well, I'm not particularly wanted around here, am I?

PATSY: I thought Mum made it quite clear you were very much wanted.

NEIL: By you?

PATSY: *(Hurt)* Neil!

NEIL: I'm a fifth wheel here, and you know it.

PATSY: That's not true.

NEIL: *(Gathering momentum)* Every time I touch you, you jump as if I were some sort of fiend or something.

PATSY: Neil, how can you say that? I...

NEIL: I mean up here. Whenever we come to Sudbury it's the same old story.

PATSY: But...

NEIL: *(A new tack; urgently)* Pat, listen to me: pack your bag and come back to New York with me right now. Let's forget we ever made this stinking trip.

PATSY: *(Swamped)* Neil, I can't.

NEIL: You've got to choose eventually, Pat, and maybe today's the day. Are you an adult or a child? Are you a wife or a daughter?

PATSY: *(Stubbornly)* Both.

NEIL: *(Starting for the door)* Okay; I'm going.

PATSY: *(Frantic)* Please, Neil, don't leave now.

NEIL: I'll be at home. You can let me know when you've made up your mind. *(With somewhat elaborate nonchalance)* I'll wait a reasonable length of time.

PATSY: Please! This is Pop's weekend.

NEIL: *(With heavy sarcasm)* I'll say it is.

PATSY: What I mean is...I don't think you realize how important this lake thing is to him.

NEIL: No, I guess I don't.

PATSY: He's terribly upset, and it's just plain unfair for us to add our problems to what he's got already. He deserves some consideration.

NEIL: I'm terribly upset too. How about some consideration for me?

PATSY: Neil, if I never ask another thing of you, please stay. Just till tomorrow. Then…

NEIL: Then what?

PATSY: We'll work things out. It'll be all right. You'll see.

NEIL: I'll stay if you promise me…

PATSY: *(Quickly)* Anything, Neil. (HE *goes to embrace her. Tense,* SHE *lets him only kiss her cheek, awkwardly.* SHE *slips away. Covering her embarrassment*) If Mum is looking for me, I'll be in my room. (*Noticing* NEIL'S *glare, in a small apologetic voice*) Our room.

NEIL: *(Coldly)* I'll tell her.

PATSY: *(At the door, pleading)* And, Neil, go with Pop this afternoon.

NEIL: I'll see.

PATSY *waits a moment, but this is all the concession* SHE *is getting.* SHE *goes out through the parlor.* NEIL *crosses to the cupboard, pours a small drink, looks for ice, cannot find it, remembers there is none.*

NEIL: *(Muttering to himself)* What a household!

HE *wanders to the window, sipping his drink. Something attracts his attention through the window.* HE *goes swiftly to the outside door, arriving just as someone knocks. Immediately* HE *opens the door, admitting a thoroughly surprised* OLIVER PURDY.

NEIL: Hello!

OLIVER: Oh…er…Connor.

HE *hesitates at the doorway, quite unnerved.*

NEIL: Come in.

OLIVER *comes in, cautiously wanders across the room, looking about.*

OLIVER: Nobody home?

NEIL: Well, I'm home.

OLIVER: *(Trying, unsuccessfully, to be cheery)* Of course. I can see that, Mr. Connor.

NEIL: Call me "Neil," Mr. Purdy.

OLIVER: Yes.

NEIL: Miss Emily is in the kitchen. And my wife is upstairs, I think.

OLIVER: And the Judge?

NEIL: He's gone to the village. He hasn't got back yet.

OLIVER: Yes; he telephoned me from the village. He…er…asked me to come over right away and…uh…meet him here.

NEIL: Then, I dare say he'll be along any moment.

OLIVER: Yes. *(Trying to sound resolute)* Well, I'll just walk about outside.

NEIL: Sit down, Mr. Purdy. Make yourself at home. Please.

OLIVER: Well...er...

HE *perches uncomfortably on the edge of an easy chair.*

NEIL: Can I fix you a drink?

OLIVER: Oh, no, thank you...uh... Neil. I had to give it up six years ago. Ulcer, you know.

NEIL: I'm sorry to hear that.

OLIVER: *(Beginning to feel more at ease)* Oh, it doesn't bother me now. I'm careful, you see.

NEIL: Yes, I see. Well, that's good, isn't it?

OLIVER: Yes.

And that closes out that subject. There is a pause. OLIVER *gets up and, somewhat furtively, takes a magazine from the cobbler's bench, then returns to his chair.* NEIL, *eyeing* HIM *from across the room, smiles mischievously, lights a cigarette.*

NEIL: *(Deliberately casual)* I'm sorry to hear about that property of yours being sold.

OLIVER: *(Startled)* Property of mine?

NEIL: On Deacon's Pond.

OLIVER: No, that wasn't my property, Neil.

NEIL: I know, but...

OLIVER: My land doesn't go down to the lake. Only a couple of acres, you know. But Judge Gorse has a piece at the lower end with a boathouse, which he is kind enough to let me use. The property you were speaking of belonged to the Winfield family.

NEIL: Ah, yes: Bud Winfield.

OLIVER: Well, that's what his friends called him. Actually, his given name was Warren, Warren Winfield.

NEIL: Oh, I see.

OLIVER: He had a little sort of camp there. Not his home; that was on the other side of town. Used it to fish from, you know, and for occasional weekends. It's a nice piece of land, about a hundred and seventy-five acres. There's good partridge cover and an alder swamp. Some woodcock in there in the fall. The property runs right up over the crest of Copp's Hill. Lovely view from there.

HE *loses himself in the contemplation of it.*

NEIL: Really?

OLIVER: *(Still dreaming)* Oh, yes. *(Coming to)* Well, poor Mr. Winfield passed away last February.

NEIL: I'm sorry to hear that.

OLIVER: Very sick man. Heart, you know.

NEIL: Oh.

OLIVER: Yes. He passed on, and his sons inherited the property. Well, they didn't see fit to keep it in the family; so...

NEIL: Perhaps they just don't care about fishing.

OLIVER: That's not all there is to it, Neil. No, I'm afraid there's bad blood in that family.

NEIL: Oh?

OLIVER: Not Mr. Winfield, mind you. Very fine stock, the Winfields. *(Confidentially)* But his wife – French, you know. Actually, Franco-Italian, from around Nice somewhere. Sort of a cross-breed, you see: not fish nor fowl.

NEIL: *(Playing along with* HIM*)* Ah!

OLIVER: She died some years ago. Seemed like a nice enough woman; but nobody really knew very much about her, and I suspect...

NEIL: *(Somewhat icily)* What do you suspect, Mr. Purdy?

OLIVER: *(Sufficiently involved not to notice* NEIL's *tone)* Well, you know these foreigners. They have different standards from ours. Not the same values at all. Now, if she'd been of the nobility, that might have been another matter. But she wasn't, Neil. Pretended to have some sort of title in her background; but it was Bonapartist, I'm sure. No; basically, Neil, she was low class.

NEIL: Low class.

OLIVER: Yes; yes. If it didn't show much on her, it certainly turned up in her sons. Blood will tell, my boy; blood will tell.

NEIL: Oh come now, Purdy; you were a business man. What has blood got to do with buying or selling anything? Before you made out a policy, you didn't ask if your client's ancestors came over on the Mayflower, did you?

OLIVER: That's quite another story, Neil. An insurance policy is not something handed down to me by my father and my grandfather. It isn't a sacred trust. Its sale has no effect whatever on my neighbors and their enjoyment. Quite another story. I think you can see that.

NEIL: Well, I don't see what's "low class" about selling what you don't need and don't want to whatever party makes the best offer. I should think that would be in the grand tradition of American free enterprise.

OLIVER: *(Sharply)* Young man, if you don't see what's wrong with introducing a lot of vulgar, good-for-nothing people into a community of respectable gentlefolk, then I have nothing more to say to you.

HE *buries himself in his magazine.* NEIL *freshens his drink; then, unable to let the matter drop:*

NEIL: Mr. Purdy, I believe you just want to hog that fishing to yourself. You just don't want anybody else on that lake.

OLIVER: *(Not looking up from His magazine)* I have nothing more to say to you.

NEIL: You'd have had the same objections if Mr. Coates had bought the property.

OLIVER: *(Looking up; grandly)* I suppose you don't think Burnham Coates is vulgar because he happens to be rich and owns some fancy art work, which his agents have bought for him. Well, his paternal grandfather was what they called in those days a common drummer, and his mother's family were nothing but Irish immigrants.

NEIL: *(Very evenly)* You know, I think in your book anybody is vulgar who deigns to disagree with Oliver Purdy.

OLIVER: *(Sanctimoniously)* Let the chips fall where they may, Mr. Connor.

OLIVER *returns to his magazine.* NEIL *gulps down his drink and, with a shrug of his shoulders, saunters out the window.* OLIVER, *left alone, is rattled. His hands shake and his knuckles whiten as* HE *grips his magazine. Suddenly* HE *throws it to the floor, furiously, and buries his head in his hand. Presently, the* JUDGE *enters from the parlor, full of energy and in good spirits.* HE *carries a book and some papers.* OLIVER *looks up. The* JUDGE *acknowledges his presence without noting his condition and proceeds directly to the table.*

JUDGE: Ah, I'm glad you're here, Ollie. I've got some good news for you.

OLIVER: *(Hoarsely)* Really?

JUDGE: Cheer up, boy, cheer up! The old Judge has been doing his homework, and everything's going to be daisy. We've got Mr. Hapgood and his amusement park right where the hair is short. *(NEIL appears at the window)* Good morning, Neil.

NEIL: 'Morning, Judge.

JUDGE: Excuse us, my boy, we've got some business to attend to.

NEIL: Oh, sure.

HE *turns as though to go out again.*

JUDGE: No, no; you don't have to go. Take a seat; this just might interest you. Come over here, Ollie, and have a look at this.

The JUDGE *opens the book and spreads the papers out on the table.*

OLIVER: What is it, Cal?

HE *settles himself on the bench opposite the* JUDGE.

JUDGE: Do you remember during the war there was talk of that factory locating here? Made some silly damn thing like hub-caps or radio tubes; I don't just recall what.

OLIVER: Tubes. That's what it was. But not the whole tube, I think; just the filament or...

JUDGE: Well, whatever the hell. They wanted to set this plant up in the meadow on the other side of Copp's Hill?

OLIVER: I remember.

JUDGE: Then you may also remember how the town fathers got themselves all worked up about it. War effort or no war effort, Sudbury wasn't going to be turned into a mill town. Its value to the country, if any, was as a residential area and a scenic spot for vacationists. So they slapped through a zoning law covering all this section of the township, including Deacon's Pond.

HE *spreads out a map before* OLIVER *and designates the appropriate area.*

OLIVER: I see what you're driving at, Cal, but I don't think we can get Hapgood on a zoning violation. He isn't planning to put up a factory on the pond – at least, I hope not, and that's all the law applies to.

JUDGE: You think so? Maybe that was the original intention; but, at the town meeting when the zoning committee made its proposals, they got so scared that somebody would find a loop-hole they began piling up specifications from here to hell-and-gone.

OLIVER: So?

NEIL, *across the room, begins to pay closer attention.*

JUDGE: So take a look at this from the 1943 Town Record. *(HE hands OLIVER an open book. As OLIVER reads)* I thought at the time they were only making damn fools of themselves. Didn't pay much attention then; but, in bed last night, some of those old phrases began popping into my mind. *(Leaning over OLIVER, HE points out the pertinent passages. NEIL rises)* This stuff here restricting the use of steel construction. And here, limiting the height of buildings to thirty-five feet above ground level.

OLIVER: *(Somewhat impatiently; trying to read)* Yes, yes.

JUDGE: Sort of throws out the idea of a Ferris wheel, doesn't it?

A pause as OLIVER *reads.* NEIL *begins to drift towards them.*

OLIVER: *(The light dawning)* Ye-e-s!

JUDGE: Now get a load of this: *(Pointing to another section)* Restrictions on the use of heavy machinery. *(And another)* Restrictions on excessive noise. What, pray, does that do to Mr. Hapgood's merry-go-round? Or his midway?

OLIVER: Kind of puts the kibosh on 'em doesn't it, Cal?

JUDGE: *(With mock gravity)* I think so.

OLIVER: I'm greatly relieved, greatly relieved.

NEIL *has come up behind* OLIVER, *who, suddenly aware of* HIM, *begins nervously to clear his throat.*

JUDGE: What's the matter, Ollie?

OLIVER: Cal, I...er...suddenly remembered: Augusta's having some people in for lunch...

JUDGE: Well, you can stay a while yet, can't you?

OLIVER: *(Rising, avoiding NEIL)* No, really. You see she's planned an early meal, and... *(Going to the window)* Look, Cal, I'm very grateful to you and very much relieved.

JUDGE: Ollie, I sort of hoped we might talk over strategy, you know.

OLIVER: Oh, I trust you completely, Cal. However you want to go about it will suit me just fine.

JUDGE: But, Ollie...

OLIVER: I'll give you a call this evening and find out how the fishing went. And, Cal, I mean it: I'm very grateful.

And HE *has gone. The* JUDGE *is flabbergasted.*

JUDGE: Well, that's the by-God-est performance! *(*NEIL *grunts assent)* I'm afraid you've upset him. He doesn't like you, you know.

NEIL: I know. And, quite frankly, I must admit the reaction is reciprocal.

JUDGE: *(With a sigh)* Oh, Neil. (HE *goes over to the cobbler's bench to putter with his fishing tackle. After a pause)* Were you baiting him?

NEIL: We had words.

JUDGE: *(As before)* Oh, Neil.

NEIL: I'm sorry. But I'd be more sorry if I had to have words with you as well.

JUDGE: What do you mean?

NEIL: Do you share Mr. Purdy's point of view?

JUDGE: I should say that Oliver and I were in general agreement. Yes.

NEIL: Gee, I was hoping you wouldn't say that.

JUDGE: Oh? Just what is his point of view, Neil – as you see it?

NEIL: He was talking, before you came, as though that lake were your and his private preserve.

JUDGE: Well, it isn't, of course.

NEIL: Mr. Purdy doesn't even have property on it.

JUDGE: Anyone can use the pond. There's public access.

NEIL: According to Mr. Purdy, that "anybody" has to be white, Anglo-Saxon, Protestant...

JUDGE: Oh, come on, Neil, did Oliver say that?

NEIL: Not in so many words.

JUDGE: *(With a shrug)* Well, then.

HE *goes back to his puttering; takes a book from the cobbler's bench and looks for a place for it on the shelves.*

NEIL: You're not taking me very seriously.

JUDGE: I think you're taking yourself seriously enough for two.

NEIL: *(Trying to control his temper)* I believe I have a right to feel serious concern when I hear Hitlerism expounded in the sovereign state of Connecticut in this year of grace, Nineteen hundred and–

JUDGE: *(Facing* NEIL, *having found a place for his book; gently)* Hitlerism?

NEIL: *(Sharply)* Yes.

JUDGE: Race stuff?

NEIL: Mm.

A pause while the JUDGE *decides what approach to take.* HE *will give whimsy another try.*

JUDGE: Well, what's wrong with white, Anglo-Saxon, Protestants?

NEIL: *(Exploding)* What's wrong with low-class, Irish Catholic immigrants?

JUDGE: *(Deciding at last to take* NEIL *seriously)* I see. *(After a moment to collect his thoughts,* HE *proceeds to compose a lecture)* Neil, I hope you will believe me that I defer to no one in my abhorrence of the late Mr. Hitler's anthropological theories. I understand that any respectable scholar in the field will tell you that, one, no racial group is inherently superior – whatever that means – to any other and, two, few people can claim racial purity – whatever that is in any case.

NEIL: I'm glad you believe that, Judge; but Mr. Purdy...

JUDGE: *(Snapping)* Don't interrupt me, young man.

NEIL: I'm sorry.

JUDGE: To say as much is not to deny that I am proud of my particular ancestry. I'm glad I am not a Chinaman or a Zulu; but, if I were a Chinaman or a Zulu, I should like to think I'd be no more ashamed of my progenitors than indeed I am.

NEIL: Hmm.

JUDGE: Now, because I am not ashamed – because, in fact, I respect and revere my heritage, I prefer to associate with others who share it. I'm comfortable with them. We speak the same language – and I don't mean a language of words only. I can express myself, fulfill myself through them; and they, through me. All right?

NEIL: Yes, but...

JUDGE: *(Plowing on)* For the same reason, I enjoy being with a lawyer, or a collector of antiques, or, especially, as you can well imagine – a fisherman. We have the same enthusiasms; we understand each other. If a man shares my addiction to the murdering of small-mouthed bass, he's my friend; and I don't give a damn if he's an Irishman, a Jew, or a Cherokee. *(*NEIL *tries to get a word in, unsuccessfully)* For Oliver Purdy, of course, I cannot speak; but I think he would, in general, subscribe to these opinions.

NEIL: I rather think not, Judge. He's not quite as temperate as you; in fact...

JUDGE: Not in speech, perhaps.

NEIL: Not in speech, most definitely.

JUDGE: Dear boy, before you judge, you'd do well to understand.

NEIL: Hmm?

JUDGE: Once upon a time, Oliver Purdy was an attractive young man with a good job, a beautiful wife, and every prospect for a happy future. All they wanted, Augusta and he, to make life perfect was a child; and, at last, after nine years of false alarms and miscarriages, a child arrived, a son. The birth was difficult, and Augusta was told the baby would have to be her last; but, no matter: the boy was in fine shape. When he was six months old, a servant – an Irish girl, you may be interested to learn – left him in his carriage while she stopped to gossip with a friend. She neglected to set the brake securely, and the carriage, being at the top of a slight incline, began to roll. Before anyone could stop it, it careened off the sidewalk and crashed into a wall. The baby was thrown out, struck on the head, and instantly killed.

NEIL: Oh.

JUDGE: After that, Augusta went to pieces. Blamed herself for failing Oliver, blamed Oliver for failing her – I don't know; at any rate, she became a chronic invalid and a scarcely tolerable scold. Along the way, the doctors have taken most of Oliver's savings; and now his own health has begun to deteriorate, and he is unemployable. His hopes are dust; his promises are ashes. He's sick, lonely, broke, and – do you wonder? – bitter.

NEIL: Other men have suffered.

JUDGE: And they are bitter, too. Don't ask for saints, Neil. They're the bonus, not the paycheck, we get for living in this world.

NEIL: You think your little scheme is going to soothe Mr. Purdy's bitterness?

JUDGE: I sincerely hope so.

NEIL: And that zoning law will really keep Hapgood off the lake?

JUDGE: I believe it will.

NEIL: I can't imagine a man like Hapgood not making sure of such things in advance. He must know all about your zoning law, and his councilors must have advised him that it's safe to go ahead.

JUDGE: I'd be amazed if they have. Amusement parks, I realize, are not specifically mentioned in the law, but the stipulations certainly rule out...

NEIL: You don't even know what kind of amusement park he has in mind.

JUDGE: What kinds are there?

NEIL: Well...

JUDGE: Neil, I'm quite sanguine about the whole affair. It doesn't really matter whether Mr. Hapgood's lawyers have found what they think is a loophole or not.

NEIL: Oh?

JUDGE: Ultimately the interpretation of the law is up to the town meeting. If the town decides that the park is undesirable, the sale just won't be...er... "finalized" is, I think, the unfortunate word in current usage.

NEIL: And the town will decide against it?

JUDGE: I think so. I'm not accustomed to throwing my weight around, Neil; but, if it's necessary, I have the weight to throw. You understand?

NEIL: It sounds as if you're telling me you've...well... "bought" the town.

JUDGE: *(Indignantly)* Certainly not! But I hope I've earned the town's respect after all these years. To most of the people here, Deacon's Pond means much the same as it means to me. If some of them are inclined to forget that, it will be pretty easy for me to remind them.

NEIL: So Mr. Hapgood hasn't a chance?

JUDGE: Very little, I should say.

NEIL: That darn lake must mean an awful lot.

JUDGE: It does, Neil. This evening I hope you'll discover that for yourself. We have a date, haven't we?

NEIL: Have we?

JUDGE: I hope so. It's been on my calendar a long time, Neil.

NEIL: I'll tell you what, Judge; I'll make a deal with you.

JUDGE: Oh, no; I'm not making any bargains. If you don't want to go, I'm not interested in...

Abruptly, HE *crosses up to the table to collect the map, papers, etc., left there.*

NEIL: Please hear me out.

A short pause as the JUDGE *busies* HIMSELF *at the table.*

JUDGE: Well, what is it then?

NEIL: If I try to find out what Deacon's Pond means to you, won't you try to find out what it might mean to Mr. Hapgood and his customers?

JUDGE: Of course I... What do you want me to do?

NEIL: See Hapgood. Let him state his case. You don't really know what he has in mind. You don't really know what sort of a man he is.

JUDGE: I can guess.

NEIL: So can I, Judge. But that's not the point. In court, do you condemn a man because you guess he's guilty? Presumably, you know he is – or, at any rate, you're convinced by the facts beyond the peradventure of a doubt. I'm only asking you to suspend judgment until you have at least a few facts to go on.

JUDGE: Will you suspend judgment too, Neil?

A pause.

NEIL: Yes. I will.

JUDGE: Perhaps I can locate Hapgood today. I think he lives in Wethersford. Maybe he can come over tomorrow.

NEIL: It's a deal then. I'll be with you on the lake this afternoon.

JUDGE: It's a deal.

CURTAIN

ACT TWO
Scene One

Deacon's Pond. Late afternoon of the same day. In the foreground, extending from S.R. towards the center of the stage, is a portion of a small island, a tangle of low-lying shrubs and marsh grasses and, at the water's edge, reeds and aquatic plants. Mid-stage, extending from S.L., is a finger of land, the tip of a peninsula stretching from the invisible off-stage shore. It is grassed and reeded like the island, but a few frail saplings S.L. suggest a more substantial tree growth beyond at the peninsula's base. A prospect of the further shore is visible S.R. – birches at the water's edge, heavier growth inland – curving upstage as though into the distance. The sun is low in the west (R.), but has not yet set. A golden light splashes the trees and the waters of the lake. During the scene, the light gradually pales; a mist rises, swallowing up the further prospect.

A rowboat is anchored upstage of the spit of land S.L., parallel to the shore, its bow pointing R. NEIL *is seated at the oars. The* JUDGE *stands in the bow with a light fishing rod, making short expert casts toward the peninsula shore. The only sound is the swish of his line. He casts once, twice. A bird call is heard overhead, quite clearly at first, scarcely discernible on repetition. The* JUDGE *looks up, following the flight of the unseen bird.*

JUDGE: Wood duck. *(*NEIL *squints up – too late. The* JUDGE *casts again)* You see how it's done. Very simple really. All with the wrist. There. *(*HE *completes the cast)* Want to try?

NEIL: Do you trust me?

JUDGE: Why not?

NEIL: I lost that big one up the way.

JUDGE: Oh, he wasn't so big.

NEIL: He was a monster.

JUDGE: Your cast was pretty good, but you got jumpy when he came for the fly; you jerked it out of his mouth. Take it easy; that's the story. Here.

HE *hands* NEIL *the rod.*

NEIL: Okay.

JUDGE: Just stand up where you are. Easy does it now.

NEIL *draws the oars back through the oarlocks and rises. The* JUDGE *sits in the bow.* NEIL *casts, earnestly biting his nether lip.*

JUDGE: You're still casting with your whole arm. Don't bend your elbow. Just a flick of the wrist.

NEIL: I'll get it.

JUDGE: Of course you will. You're stripping out too much line.

NEIL: *(Impatiently)* All right. All right. *(*HE *casts again. The line is too long, and the fly hits the shore, tangling in the reeds)* Shoot!

JUDGE: I told you you had too much line.

NEIL: I know you did. I'm sorry.

JUDGE: Nothing to be sorry about. *(HE tugs on the line, but cannot free it)* We'd better pull into shore; it's really snarled up.

NEIL: That sort of creams this spot.

JUDGE: We don't catch much here anyway. *(NEIL works the boat into shore with the upstage oar. The JUDGE reaches out and disentangles the line)* There we go.

NEIL: I'm awfully sorry; really I am.

JUDGE: Forget it. *(Undoing a knot in the line)* There. Want to get out on shore? Stretch our legs a bit?

NEIL: I'd like to. That seat's pretty hard.

HE *steps gingerly ashore. The* JUDGE *reaches up to help* HIM.

JUDGE: That's not a problem with my fat ass.

HE *gets out of the boat.* NEIL *helps* HIM *ashore.*

NEIL: *(Sprawling on the grass)* I'm afraid I've spoiled your day.

JUDGE: Will you stop that nonsense, Neil.

NEIL: I'm such a bloody amateur, that's all.

JUDGE: Rome wasn't built in a day, Neil.

NEIL: How long have you been building Rome?

JUDGE: Hmm?

NEIL: How long have you been coming here?

JUDGE: Well, let's see: my grandfather brought me here the first time when I was about, I guess, seven. It's been a good many years.

NEIL: Holy cow! That means an awful lot of bass for breakfast.

JUDGE: Not as much as you might think, really. Less now than there used to be.

NEIL: Oh? What do you catch a day? As a rule, I mean.

JUDGE: Varies. One or two's about average nowadays. Lots of times we get none at all.

NEIL: Gosh, I feel even worse now about losing that one. I didn't realize they were so few and far between.

JUDGE: Oh, hell, we almost always get a nibble at least. I'd like a dollar for every one Ollie and I have lost.

NEIL: I'm in good company then?

JUDGE: Of course. Though frankly, Neil, I don't think I'd have missed that one.

NEIL: Would Mr. Purdy? *(HE takes out a pack of cigarettes and offers one to the* JUDGE*)* Cigarette?

JUDGE: *(Taking out a pipe and filling it)* No, thanks; I always smoke a pipe out here. Emmy doesn't like my smoking it around the house. You were asking about Oliver. He's pretty good, you know. Ought to be: he's been studying over thirty years with the master. A bit of a liar, though.

NEIL: Oh?

JUDGE: Not in a big way, really. It's just that Ollie's pound is fourteen ounces and his inch is one-eighth shorter than yours or mine. When he tells you how big a fish he's caught, you have to make a few mental corrections, that's all. Want to pee?

NEIL: What?

JUDGE: I'm just going over to the bushes there.

HE *rises, points off S.L.*

NEIL: Oh. No, thank you.

The JUDGE *goes off L.* NEIL *shakes his head in amusement, takes a few puffs on his cigarette, rises, and walks to the end of the point, R.* HE *stands there a moment looking over the lake.* HE *takes another puff on his cigarette and flicks it out into the water. A bird calls overhead, as at the beginning of the scene;* NEIL *looks up and follows its flight, muttering to himself.*

NEIL: Wood duck.

The JUDGE *returns.*

JUDGE: Curious satisfaction a man gets peeing out of doors. I always like to go out on the lawn after dark, though Emmy thinks it's pretty uncouth.

NEIL: A bit primitive perhaps.

JUDGE: I guess so. But I don't think it's a bad idea to revisit the cave now and again and check our present against our past.

NEIL: I know you're inclined to look back, Judge, but I didn't think you'd go that far.

JUDGE: Oh, beyond the cave, Neil. We were animals before we were men; and before that, long before that, little blobs of primordial slime. And there's still something of the animal in us and something of the blob.

NEIL: And you really want to return to the blob, eh, Judge? You know, I doubt that somehow.

JUDGE: No, not return certainly. I'm quite pleased to be a man. But it's a good idea, I think, to recognize the blob and the animal within us and understand their needs so that we can take care of them. Better that than acting like animals – or blobs – when we think we're behaving like men.

NEIL: And so you go in the bushes or on the lawn after dark.

JUDGE: Exactly. It's a less ugly way of celebrating one's animalhood than, well, cavorting around an amusement park. (HE *looks upstage toward the far end of the lake*) It would sure make a mess of this lake, Neil.

NEIL: It'll certainly change it.

JUDGE: *(Abstracted)* Yes. *(Coming to)* Well, let's get back to business. Time's a wastin'.

HE *moves toward the boat.* NEIL *does not follow him.*

NEIL: Judge.

JUDGE: Hmm?

NEIL: I just want to ask you one thing: why are you so afraid of change? You of all people should be the least dismayed. After all, you've contemplated the blob that changed into the dinosaur that changed into the cave man that changed into Judge Calvin Gorse; certainly you don't expect the procession to stop suddenly after all those millions of years.

JUDGE: *(Somewhat flustered)* No, I don't, of course. I know that things have to change. *(Breaking a little)* But I...I don't want this to change, Neil. Anything but this. *(Pulling* HIMSELF *together)* You think I'm just being sentimental about this lake, don't you?

NEIL: I appreciate your feelings, Judge. They've had an awful long time to set. But when Mr. Hapgood comes tomorrow, I doubt that he's going to be much moved by your private romance with Deacon's Pond.

JUDGE: You're not moved, are you, Neil?

NEIL: As I say, I appreciate your feelings.

JUDGE: Well, just wait and see.

NEIL: What'll I see?

JUDGE: You'll see. In a matter of minutes. *(HE gets into the boat)* Come on; we'll have just about enough time to take a swipe along that island.

NEIL: *(Crossing to the boat)* Why? We've got more than an hour before dinner time, haven't we?

HE *gets into the boat and takes up the oars.*

JUDGE: But just a few minutes till the bass's bedtime.

NEIL: Huh?

HE *hasn't started to row yet, is waiting for the* JUDGE's *instructions.*

JUDGE: Just take it down off the point there. Along where those bushes hang over the water, we sometimes have a bit of luck. *(NEIL begins to work the boat S.R. and downstage)* See that hill over there?

NEIL: *(Craning* HIS *neck to look)* Yes.

JUDGE: Take it easy now. Copp's Hill we call it. The sun's just riding over the top of it now. When it goes down behind, that's when the bass call it quits.

NEIL: What do you mean?

JUDGE: They stop biting.

NEIL: How come?

JUDGE: Everybody has his own theory. Ollie thinks it has something to do with the temperature change at the water surface; others say it's an effect of the light. You pays your money, and you takes your choice. *(THEY are above the island, just right of center stage)* Lift oars now: we'll drift along here. *(HE *takes up the rod and rises, begins to strip off some line)* You don't mind if I work this stretch? It's a bit tricky.

NEIL: Go ahead.

JUDGE: *(As* HE *begins to fish)* No; I could count on the fingers of one hand the number of rises we've got after the sun's gone behind Copp's Hill. Since I've been coming here, four or five mavericks; that's all.

NEIL: Strange.

JUDGE: Yes. The magic moment.

NEIL: Magic?

JUDGE: *(Somewhat mysteriously)* You'll see. *(*NEIL *is amused and a little perplexed, but decides to pursue the matter no further; pause. The* JUDGE *continues to fish)* We're drifting a little bit too fast. Brake it with your left oar. *(*NEIL *dips the upstage oar. The boat, which has been moving toward S.R. almost imperceptibly, moves even more slowly)* Gently does it. You know, you're a pretty good boatman.

NEIL: Thanks.

JUDGE: After all these years, Emmy still can't tell her right oar from her left. Otherwise, she's pretty good. *(A pause.* HE *casts again)* Actually this particular stretch has been slim pickin's this summer. Used to be one of the best spots in the lake, but it's been falling off now for several years. I don't know what's happened.

NEIL: Why do you fish it then?

JUDGE: Oh, we like to check all the places. You never can tell when something may crop up. *(*HE *reels in)* No dice. Let's go along just past that clump of reeds. See? One pull of the oars should do it. *(*NEIL *puts the oars in the water)* Take it real easy now. *(*NEIL *pulls gently on the oars; the boat lunges a few feet to far S.R.)* Whoa! Brake it, boy; brake it. *(*NEIL *sets the oars rather abruptly. The* Judge *speaks rather sharply)* Take it easy, I said. If you stir it up like that, you'll scare hell out of every bass in the lake.

NEIL: *(Meekly)* I'm sorry.

JUDGE: *(Gently)* That's all right, my boy. It's a bad day for biting anyway. Water's too warm; we need rain. I'm surprised as hell you rose the one you did.

There is a lengthy pause as HE *begins to fish again.*

NEIL: It's fantastic.

JUDGE: You like it, eh?

NEIL: *(A bit too quickly to be fully convincing)* Oh, sure; yes. But that wasn't what I meant.

JUDGE: Oh?

NEIL: I was just thinking: you amaze me, you know?

JUDGE: I do?

NEIL: Coming out here like this, day after day, maybe catching one little fish.

JUDGE: Summer of forty-eight, I got a seven-pounder. I don't call that little.

NEIL: All right: a seven-pounder umpteen years ago. But, as you say, a lot of the time you don't get any at all.

JUDGE: Don't judge this kind of fishing, Neil, by the size of your catch. If you're looking for quantity, you'd do better at some hatchery pond. These are native smallmouths, boy. The Good Lord put them here, and He's not about to overstock any lake just to please poor greedy sinners like thee and me. He doesn't want to spoil us, you see.

NEIL: Don't you ever get the idea, once in a while, that you're settling into a rut?

JUDGE: Call it a rut, if you like. What's wrong with that?

NEIL: Variety is the spice of life.

JUDGE: At your age maybe; but I've had all the variety I want.

NEIL: Really?

JUDGE: Sure. Emily and I took a couple of trips to Europe before the war. There were two summers when I hardly had a chance to put a fly in the water. We enjoyed traveling; talked about going around the world even, after Patsy grew up. Then, when the chance came, we both felt we were just as happy here doing what we'd always done. *(A pause as* HE *casts)* Some people, Neil, seem to like uprooting themselves every few years. They switch from job to job; but they have no real profession. They move from house to house, and never have a home. They change their tastes, their ideas, their standards, always testing and discarding, never making up their minds about anything.

NEIL: Times change, though. You remember when the automobile was a newfangled contraption that everybody said was just a passing fad?

JUDGE: I certainly do.

NEIL: But you're not driving a horse and buggy these days.

JUDGE: No.

NEIL: And you're not about to trade your new Buick in for a barouche.

JUDGE: Damn right I'm not.

NEIL: Well?

JUDGE: I don't want to go back to the time when it took the better part of a day to drive into Wethersford, a trip you can make now in less than an hour. But I haven't forgotten the joy of those trips either. There was no pushing, no shoving, no hurry; fat lot of good it would do. You were stuck there behind that horse's ass, hour after hour, with nothing to do except live. And you could see every flower along the roadside, every bird sitting on every fence, every camel and whale of a cloud in the sky; and they all became part of you and part of your life forever. I may have changed my mode of transportation; but the same man who could sit for hours in that buggy and simply live is living the same way on this pond this afternoon.

NEIL: I see.

JUDGE: When I die, you won't be burying thirty-five two-year-olds or a hundred and forty six-month-old babes, but one man of seventy – or eighty, if I can make it.

NEIL: Or a billion-year-old blob.

JUDGE: Exactly. A somewhat improved – in fact, I should like to think, a rather highly developed, billion-year-old blob.

NEIL *chuckles. The* JUDGE *is reeling in.* NEIL *looks off R.*

NEIL: The sun's just a sliver on the top of the hill now.

JUDGE: Yes. And we've pretty well covered the fishing along here. Pretty much a skunk day, but I didn't really expect anything, what with no rain. It's been nice, though. Enjoy yourself?

NEIL: Sure. It would have been nicer if I'd caught that son of a bitch up the way.

JUDGE: Live and learn.

NEIL: *(Amused; to* HIMSELF*)* Live and learn.

JUDGE: Now, let's just sit and watch it happen.

NEIL: Watch what happen?

JUDGE: You'll see. In a minute now. *(*THEY *look off towards Copp's Hill)* There. See how the light is changing? There's still a patch of gold up there.

NEIL: The sun's down.

JUDGE: And now it's silver.

NEIL: Uhuh.

There is a soft, whirring sound. The grasses on the island and the peninsula move. NEIL, *with a scarcely conscious gesture, buttons his shirt collar.*

JUDGE: *(Lowering his voice)* The breeze always comes up at this hour. That's a signal.

NEIL: *(Aloud)* Signal?

JUDGE: Ssshh! *(Whispering)* Watch!

THEY *watch. In the changing light and the gathering mist, the lake is transfigured. The far shore is invisible, and the nearer landmarks are engulfed in shadow.*

JUDGE: Listen!

Mixed with the soughing of the breeze, a barely audible chirping sound, monotonous and regular.

NEIL: Peepers.

JUDGE: *(Whispering)* Listen! *(*THEY *are silent and attentive; the* JUDGE *is rapt, as though in a trance. The natural sounds become the ghostly whirring of strings.* NEIL *fidgets)* Shhh! *(A pause)* Do you hear it? *(And now, over the accompanying strings, a piping sound, as of a flute or ancient shepherd's pipe played in the far, far distance. The* JUDGE *listens;* NEIL *strains to hear)* "Come home! Come home!"; that's what it's saying.

NEIL: A bird?

JUDGE: No bird. *(A pause)* Don't you hear it now?

NEIL: *(Straining)* I think…I think…

JUDGE: *(In a tiny voice, suggesting the call of the pipe)* Come home! Come home!

He *looks at* NEIL *intently.*

NEIL: *(Trying hard to oblige)* I hear the peepers and the wind in the trees.

And that is all anyone can hear now.

JUDGE: *(Disappointed)* It's stopped now. They've all gone home.

NEIL: It's turned cold.

JUDGE: Yes. Time for us to go home too.

NEIL: Yes. I guess so.

The JUDGE *settles disconsolately in the bow seat.* NEIL *takes up the oars.*

CURTAIN

Scene Two

The living room; mid-afternoon of the following day (Sunday). JUDGE GORSE *is discovered alone, preparing the room for the arrival of the Hapgoods.* HE *is obviously somewhat nervous and tense in his anticipation.* HE *is over-meticulous in his attempts to arrange the chairs, up- and down-stage of the fireplace, moving one an inch or so this way or that, standing back to appraise its angle, and then adjusting it again. The next project is to remove the accumulation of objects from the cobbler's bench and to stash them away in the cabinet space beneath the downstage section of the bookcase. But this space is already filled to overflowing; and, when* HE *opens the cabinet doors, a pile of old magazines and boxes tumbles out. Muttering to himself,* HE *stacks the material from the cobbler's bench with the new collection from the cabinet – more or less neatly – on the floor behind the downstage easy chair, readjusting the chair to hide (somewhat) the pile. On the cobbler's bench,* HE *arranges the maps and town records* HE *was showing* OLIVER *in Act I, Scene 2. Beside them* HE *places an ashtray and the cigarette box from the dresser. As* HE *steps back to survey his work,* EMILY *enters from the parlor with a pitcher of water and ice for drinks.*

EMILY: *(Crossing to the table to set down the pitcher and ice-bucket)* I suppose they'll be wanting drinks.

JUDGE: Mm.

HE *has discovered that the cigarette box is empty and crosses to the dresser to rummage through its drawers.*

EMILY: What are you looking for?

JUDGE: Where have we hidden the cigarettes?

EMILY: There aren't any. We ran out last night.

JUDGE: Oh, no!

EMILY: Now, don't fuss about it, dear. Neil has gone into town to get some.

JUDGE: *(Appreciatively)* Ah, you think of everything, Emmy.

EMILY: I try. *(Amused,* SHE *watches the* JUDGE, *who is arranging chairs again)* What on earth are you doing?

JUDGE: Hmm?

EMILY: Pushing those chairs around as if you were planning to receive the Queen of England.

JUDGE: Oh, that reminds me: the Queen – I mean his wife. I didn't really figure on her coming.

EMILY: Patsy and I will take care of her. Show her around, while you men get down to business.

JUDGE: I'm sorry to impose upon you, Em. I don't know what she's like. Cookie Cuthbert in all probability.

EMILY: I'll be quite safe. I doubt somehow that she'll convert me into a strip teaser. *(The* JUDGE *opens the "Town Record" to the appropriate pages rearranging it on the cobbler's bench. As* SHE *crosses to the cupboard)* Would you like a drink, dear?

JUDGE: You're offering me a drink?

EMILY: *(Getting out the bourbon)* It might relax you a little.

JUDGE: Relax?

EMILY: *(Fixing a drink for* HIM*)* I don't know what's the matter with you, Cal. You've been moody all day – ever since last evening, in fact. We've never played such peculiar bridge. And now, with the Hapgoods coming, you're all wound up like a watch. What's the trouble, dear?

SHE *extends the drink to him;* HE *comes to the table, takes the drink, and slumps onto the bench, sighing.*

JUDGE: Oh, Emmy, I don't know. I just don't know if I'm doing the right thing, that's all.

EMILY: Of course you are. I think it's very fair and decent of you to explain the zoning law to Mr. Hapgood face to face. Other men would have–

JUDGE: Oh, that! That was Neil's idea.

EMILY: Give the devil his due. It should have been yours.

JUDGE: That's not what's bothering me. I mean the whole business of the zoning law: I'm not sure it'll hold water,

EMILY: But it's against amusement parks, isn't it?

JUDGE: Not exactly, I'm afraid.

EMILY: No? But at least, it's meant to keep the lake…well, nice?

JUDGE: Nice for whom, Emmy?

EMILY: Well, everybody, of course.

JUDGE: Everybody's idea of "nice" isn't the same. I'm sure Mr. Hapgood thinks an amusement park is just about the nicest thing in the world; and, if he wants to make an issue of it, who's to say that a majority of the town meeting won't go along with him?

EMILY: I, for one.

JUDGE: What makes you so sure?

EMILY: Because you'll charm them into agreeing with you. You know you can do it; and, what's more, I know you have every intention of doing it.

JUDGE: Maybe I could. And I had every intention; but now, I–

EMILY: Calvin Gorse! As long as I've known you, I've heard nothing but Deacon's Pond and how much it means to you. To hear you talk, it's as though that lake was some kind of religion for you.

JUDGE: It is that, Emmy.

EMILY: Then don't tell me, after all these years, you're not going to fight for it now.

JUDGE: Well, I've been doing some thinking. You take Neil, for example.

EMILY: *(Impatiently)* Neil!

JUDGE: Just a sec, Emmy. Whatever you think about that young man, you'll have to admit he's a cultivated fellow. He's sensitive. He's got good taste.

EMILY: *(Conceding, for sake of the argument)* All right.

JUDGE: Well yesterday afternoon, out there on Deacon's Pond–

EMILY: He had a very good time.

JUDGE: What makes you think so?

EMILY: He told me he did.

JUDGE: *(Brightening)* Did he now? *(Glum again)* Well, he didn't tell me.

HE *rises and moves R. taking his drink with* HIM.

EMILY: He should have. But you have to face it, dear: Neil is just not a very considerate boy.

JUDGE: *(Pursuing his own line of thought)* I suppose he found the experience pleasant enough; but obviously the lake didn't really mean very much to him.

EMILY: Why should it, dear? Neil isn't a fisherman. You can't expect him to feel about the lake the way you do. I don't feel that way either. It's a nice place, and I enjoy going out there with you once in a while. But I'm not devoted to Deacon's Pond; it's not the be-all and end-all of my life. You know it isn't, and you don't expect it to be.

JUDGE: I don't expect you to share my feelings, Emily; but I do expect you to understand them.

EMILY: And I do.

JUDGE: As far as Neil is concerned, I'm just some sort of old crank.

EMILY: Neil hasn't known you as long as I have. And he hasn't lived your kind of life.

JUDGE: Very few people, I'm afraid, have lived my kind of life. Very few that are still alive, that is.

EMILY: Very few have had your luck, Cal. You picked the right father and the right grandfather, too.

JUDGE: Hell, I'm not talking about money, Emmy! On a quarter of my income, we'd be living pretty much the same way. We'd have to do without a few small luxuries, but not enough to make much difference. I'd have to work more and loaf less; but it would be the same kind of work and the same kind of loafing. Burnham Coates is rich as Croesus, but, on most matters, we wouldn't see eye to eye together in a month of Sundays. Steve Yankovitch's father lived in a tar-paper shack, and yet we spoke the same language all the way down the line. There are farmers in this township I understand better and who understand me better than my own son-in-law. But they're dying out, Emily. There are damn few of them left any more.

Moodily, HE *sets his drink down on the dresser.* OLIVER *appears at the window, taps on the glass.*

OLIVER: May I come in?

EMILY: *(Startled)* Oliver!

JUDGE: *(Somewhat diffidently, crossing to the easy chair, upstage R., and sitting in it)* Come on in, Ollie.

OLIVER: *(Coming into the room; quite bright and perky)* Our friend Hapgood hasn't arrived yet?

EMILY: We expect them any moment now.

OLIVER: Them?

JUDGE: He's bringing his wife, I think.

OLIVER: *(Curious about the* JUDGE's *evident moodiness)* Oh, I see. *(Brightly again)* Well, it's all right if I stay?

JUDGE: Sure; sure. I expected you to be here. I think, Ollie, though...if it's all right with you...I should do most of the talking.

OLIVER: You're the legal man, Cal; you should do *all* the talking. I want only to be an innocent onlooker. I just want to hear you lay down the law to those Hapgoods.

JUDGE: *(Abstractedly)* Ah, yes.

EMILY: Can I get something for you, Ollie? Some iced tea perhaps?

OLIVER: Oh, no thank you, Emily. *(Returning to his concern)* Cal, what's bothering you?

JUDGE: *(Innocently)* What do you mean? Everything's fine.

OLIVER: Come now, Cal. Yesterday you were loaded for bear; now you're sitting there as if the fight were all out of you.

JUDGE: I'm just relaxing. Right, Emmy?

EMILY: He didn't sleep very well last night. I think it was the cake he had before we went to bed.

OLIVER: Old iron constitution cracking up at last, eh?

JUDGE: No, Ollie; the constitution's great. Emily's just making up excuses for me.

OLIVER: *(Alarmed)* Look, Cal, is there something wrong about that zoning law? Will it work? *(Pause)* Tell me, please. I can take it.

JUDGE: I'm pretty sure it will work. I mean it could work if we wanted to push it.

OLIVER: *(More upset)* Well, we are going to push it, aren't we?

JUDGE: I guess so.

OLIVER: *(Exploding)* You guess! *(Turning to* HER, *desperately)* Emily, what has got into this man?

JUDGE: *(Rising, crossing to* OLIVER*)* I'm sorry, Ollie; I've been in the dumps. Call it a failure of nerve, if you will.

OLIVER: See here, Calvin, if your nerve fails, where does that leave me?

JUDGE: I understand, Ollie. Don't worry about it; everything will go according to plan.

OLIVER: Well, I should hope so.

JUDGE: I just got brooding this morning, that's all. *(Crossing away)* I began to feel...I don't know just how to put it without sounding like a goddam fool... I began to feel as if I were part of a minority somehow. As much of a minority as if my skin were black.

OLIVER: You are in a minority group, Cal. But you're not alone there; I'm with you.

JUDGE: Yes, of course. You know what I mean then?

OLIVER: Certainly.

JUDGE: But I don't know what I mean myself. It isn't as if we were being persecuted. We're not excluded from public washrooms; we're...

OLIVER: *(Forcefully)* What do you mean "we're not being excluded"? Have you ever gone into the lavatory at the Sudbury Station? *(to* EMILY*)* Pardon me, Emily; but I'm trying to make a point.

EMILY: Go right ahead, Ollie; I understand.

JUDGE: Well, as a matter of fact, I have. I made the mistake once – under the pressure of an extreme emergency.

OLIVER: Well then, you were excluded – or you have been ever since your "mistake."

JUDGE: Oh, not exactly... I...

OLIVER: *(With great conviction)* Exactly. All right, there wasn't a sign on the door saying, "Gorse and Purdy Keep Out," but there might just as well have been. That place is such a filthy, stinking... I'm sorry, Emily.

EMILY: The ladies' room isn't much better.

OLIVER: There you are. "Dirty People Only." That's what the sign would say if they had to paint one. Don't you see, Cal?

JUDGE: Yes, I see; but...

OLIVER: And it's precisely the same situation with Deacon's Pond. We're being excluded, and don't you think for a minute we're not.

JUDGE: *(Not fully convinced)* Yes, Ollie. *(After a moment of rumination)* What do you think, Emmy?

EMILY: You know what I think, dear.

JUDGE: You agree with Oliver?

OLIVER: Of course, she agrees.

EMILY: Well, I'm not sure, Ollie. I don't know quite how you got onto this minority business. It isn't as though we were living in a ghetto. If we are, it's certainly a very comfortable one.

OLIVER: *(Pompously)* It's a ghetto; that's what it is. Comfortable or not, it's a ghetto.

Having, to his satisfaction, made his point, OLIVER *struts over to the window and stands there, looking out.*

EMILY: Well, anyway, I think what's troubling you, Cal, is that you've never had to fight for what you believed in before. The kind of life you wanted was the kind you always had. What you valued most were the things most people valued. Now times have changed: others don't seem to care about what is very important to you. If it is still important, then you have to assert yourself. And that's hard, I know, if you've never had to do it till now.

OLIVER: It's easy enough for those black boys in the South. They have all sorts of committees down there fighting for their rights. It's about time we had a little fighting committee of our own.

The JUDGE *looks over at* OLIVER, *who maintains his stance at the window, a frail Napoleon surveying his empire with smug satisfaction. The* JUDGE *smiles, amused and also pitying.* HE *returns his attention to* EMILY.

JUDGE: Emmy.

EMILY: Yes, dear?

JUDGE: What I think is important – you still care about that too, don't you?

EMILY: You don't have to ask me that, Cal.

JUDGE: *(Very gently)* No. I guess I don't.

HE *takes* EMILY *in his arms and kisses* HER *on the forehead.* OLIVER *feels rather the intruder.*

OLIVER: *(Stepping out through the window)* I think I'll take a little turn around outside.

EMILY: *(To the* JUDGE*)* Why don't you go with Oliver, dear? I'll call you when the Hapgoods arrive.

JUDGE: Yes. A bit of a walk might do me good.

SHE *gives* HIM *a pat;* HE *goes out.*

JUDGE: Wait up, Ollie; I'll go along with you.

HE *joins* OLIVER *outside.* OLIVER *takes* HIM *by the arm and immediately begins chattering.*

OLIVER: Say, Cal. I heard about a new candy this morning: Chummy-Nums. It isn't alliterative, of course, but I thought the name was nauseating enough to qualify for our collection.

The JUDGE *laughs as* THEY *round the corner of the house together and are out of sight and hearing.* EMILY *looks after* THEM *a moment, then turns* HER *attention to the room, noticing the pile of boxes and papers which the* JUDGE *has left behind the chair.*

EMILY: *(More amused than exasperated)* Oh, my goodness!

SHE *opens the doors of the near section of the cabinet; finds that there is no space left within; takes the pile to another cabinet section, where* SHE *finds plenty of room to stash it away. During this operation,* NEIL *enters by the outside door.* HE *has a carton of cigarettes.*

NEIL: Got your cigarettes.

EMILY: Oh, thank you, Neil.

NEIL: *(Opening the top drawer of the dresser)* They go in here?

EMILY: Yes, please. Oh, give me a couple of packs to put in the box.

> NEIL *gives* HER *two packs from the carton and puts the opened carton away in the dresser drawer.* EMILY *empties the packs into the cigarette box.* NEIL *wanders toward the window.*

NEIL: They haven't come yet, eh?

EMILY: We expect them any time now. Your father-in-law is outside with Mr. Purdy.

NEIL: Ah, yes. *(A pause)* Where's Pat?

EMILY: *(At the same time)* Neil.

NEIL: Yes?

EMILY: I'm sorry. Patsy's upstairs, I think.

NEIL: Oh, sure; in her room. What were you going to say?

EMILY: Well, just that... I'm afraid you've rather upset the Judge.

NEIL: Not again!

EMILY: Now, Neil.

NEIL: I mean really, Miss Emily, I've been trying to be a good boy. What have I done this time?

EMILY: Nothing, except I thought you liked going out on the lake yesterday.

NEIL: I did. Very much. It's a beautiful spot. I almost caught a fish. I want to get him next time...if I get another chance.

EMILY: Why didn't you tell him that?

NEIL: The Judge? I did, didn't I? I certainly thanked him.

EMILY: He didn't think you seemed particularly enthusiastic: that's all.

NEIL: Oh, hell's bells, Miss Emily! I... Well, I guess I wasn't enthusiastic then, if you mean I didn't gush.

EMILY: I didn't say...

NEIL: Now, look here: I'm very sorry if I've disappointed the old man, but I'm afraid I'm just not the person he wants me to be. I am what I am; and I'm trying to be what *I* want to be. That's about the best I can do.

EMILY: It's the best any of us can do.

NEIL: I didn't, as they say, flip my lid about the lake, though it was thoroughly pleasant out there. But there are other things that excite me more than fishing, and they're things the Judge doesn't even want to talk about. I'm perfectly willing to meet him more than half way, but he's got to come out a little way towards me. Don't you understand?

EMILY: I understand.

NEIL: You live only for him, Miss Emily. Around this house what concerns the Judge is all that really matters.

EMILY: Oh, no; I…

NEIL: That's the way it looks to me. Perhaps it suits you; but, you see, I'm not married to him.

EMILY: Of course, you're not.

NEIL: What should I say to him then?

EMILY: Nothing you don't want to say, Neil.

NEIL: I want to say something.

EMILY: Then something nice. Anything. When you have the opportunity.

NEIL: I'll do that. I promise. *(A pause)* Patsy's upstairs, you say?

EMILY: She wanted to lie down after lunch. She may have gone to sleep. Perhaps you should wake her.

NEIL: No; I don't want to disturb her.

A pause; NEIL *is looking out the window.*

EMILY: Are you and Patsy having trouble?

NEIL: *(Guardedly)* No; of course not. *(After a pause)* Why do you ask that?

EMILY: Patsy seems upset about something.

NEIL: Patsy?

EMILY: Yes.

NEIL: She's never upset. Not when she comes here anyway. She's right at home, fussing in the kitchen with you–

EMILY: I can tell, Neil. She does the same things she always does; but, this weekend, there's a strain about her behavior, a kind of desperation, as if she were trying to get her mind off something.

NEIL: Perhaps she's worried about her father.

EMILY: She's not all that concerned about him.

NEIL: Oh? I thought he was the only thing she really was concerned about.

EMILY: Her marriage means more to her, Neil. Her marriage and you.

NEIL: You think so?

EMILY: That's the way it should be, I think.

A pause.

NEIL: You know, Miss Emily, you astonish me.

EMILY: I do?

NEIL: I'll tell you the truth now.

EMILY: I wish you would, Neil.

NEIL: I was going to leave yesterday. Leave here, that is, and, maybe, leave Patsy, leave everything.

EMILY: Oh, no. Why?

NEIL: I didn't want to exactly. I...well, you see, Miss Emily, Pat and I have been husband and wife on...er...well, you might call it an on-again-off-again relationship. (HE *pauses.* EMILY *waits for* HIM *to struggle on*) I thought we were just about getting to the point where er... things were going pretty well. But then we came up here, and it was...off again.

EMILY: What made you decide to stay?

NEIL: Three things. (*Somewhat bitterly*) First of all: we didn't want to upset the Judge in his little crisis about the lake. That's what we told ourselves anyway.

EMILY: And?

NEIL: (*After a pause*) I'm still in love with your daughter, Miss Emily.

EMILY: That makes two reasons.

NEIL: (*Hesitatingly*) Number three: I think...in a way, I didn't want to give you the satisfaction.

EMILY: Oh?

NEIL: Now you know why I said you astonished me. I thought your main objective in life – besides catering to the Judge, of course – was to break up our marriage.

EMILY: I didn't approve of you, Neil.

NEIL: I know that.

EMILY: I didn't think you'd fit in here. You don't, you know. But, you see, Patsy doesn't either.

NEIL: You do amaze me. I should have thought she'd be perfectly happy helping you look after the Judge.

EMILY: I don't need her help, Neil. I don't want it. You might say I'm a little jealous even.

NEIL: Well!

EMILY: Besides, I don't want Patsy to fall into the same trap I did. Mind you, I'm not complaining: I like my little trap very, very much. But Pat needs something different. She is a different person; and she has a different father. My father was a wonderful man in many ways. He was a scientist, you know; he invented something that goes into a radio – I never could understand it. He was brilliant, completely dedicated to his work, very strong willed, very high-principled. But he was a cold man; he never showed affection, and he never seemed to want any. Come to think of it, Neil, in many ways he was very like you.

NEIL: I don't want affection, eh?

EMILY: I said my father never *seemed* to want any. And he didn't want any of the sort I had to offer. My sister was something else again; he was devoted to her. But she was like him, you see; she became a doctor herself and a very good one, too. She could meet him on his own level, talk back to him. My, how she could tick him off! They'd go at it like cat and dog. And he loved it. He respected her, you see. But, as far as he was concerned, I was just another wishy-washy female, a brainless, useless ornament. And I'm just exactly what my husband wants. He's bright and good – as my father was – but he's so unsure of himself. He has to be told every day what a wonderful man he is. He's a baby that needs perpetual tender loving care; and that's what I'm more than happy to give. I've had a wonderful life with Cal, a life that has been full of love. But I've had to pay a price: I've had to submerge my personality completely in his; I've had to think his thoughts and dream his dreams, with never an independent idea of my own. And that just suits me right down to the ground; I don't have to fight; I don't have to compete; I don't have to shine. But it would be a terrible price for a girl like Patsy to pay; and, whatever you think you want now, Neil, I don't believe, when the chips are down, it's a price you'd ever ask. I hope I'm right, Neil. (PATSY *is at the parlor door*) Oh, here she is now. *(The doorbell rings)* And there are the Hapgoods. *(Exiting, passing* PATSY *in the doorway)* Have a nice rest, dear?

Before PATSY *can answer,* SHE *has gone.*

PATSY: Were you talking about me?

NEIL: I was just asking where you were.

PATSY: I was upstairs.

NEIL: So she told me. Did you sleep?

PATSY: I tried to.

NEIL: Pat.

PATSY *looks up at* HIM. *There is a long pause. Offstage,* EMILY *is heard answering the door and greeting the* HAPGOODS. *A jumble of voices, distant at first, then louder and clearer as the speakers approach.*

EMILY'S VOICE: Oh, hello.

HAPGOOD'S VOICE: This Gorse's place?

EMILY'S VOICE: Yes, indeed; I'm Mrs. Gorse.

HAPGOOD'S VOICE: Hapgood's the name. This is the missus.

EMILY'S VOICE: We were expecting you. Do come in. My husband will be in the living room.

MRS. HAPGOOD'S VOICE: You sure got a nice place here, Mrs. Gorse. Isn't it a nice place, Joey?

HAPGOOD'S VOICE: Yeah.

EMILY'S VOICE: Did you have trouble finding it?

HAPGOOD'S VOICE: Naw; we come right to it. We were late getting started, you see. Mother here, she just couldn't decide what dress to put on and…well, you know how it is.

MRS. HAPGOOD'S VOICE: Oh, Joey!

EMILY'S VOICE: Right in here. Watch the step there.

Meanwhile, communication between NEIL *and* PATSY *is still not possible. As the* HAPGOODS *and* EMILY *approach:*

NEIL: I better go and get your father. He's outside with the little man.

NEIL *goes out through the window, just as* MRS. HAPGOOD *appears at the parlor door,* HER *husband behind* HER *and* EMILY *bringing up the rear.* MRS. HAPGOOD *stands for a moment on the step, blocking traffic and surveying the room.*

MRS. HAPGOOD: Oh my, what a lovely room! Isn't it lovely, Joey?

SHE *turns to her husband and almost falls off the step.*

HAPGOOD: *(At the doorway)* Watch your step there, Mother, like the lady says.

MRS. HAPGOOD: *(Regaining* HER *balance)* Oh, my big feet! *(Crossing over to* PATSY*)* How are you? I'm Laurine Hapgood.

PATSY: *(Shaking* HER *proffered hand)* I'm Patsy Connor.

EMILY *and* HAPGOOD *have come into the room.* EMILY *ushers* HIM *over to* PATSY.

EMILY: This is my daughter, Mr. Hapgood.

HAPGOOD: *(Shaking* HER *hand)* Pleased to meet you, Mrs....er...

MRS. HAPGOOD: Patsy. Isn't that nice. Our daughter's name is Priscilla. She's twenty-one next week. They sure grow up fast, don't they, Mrs. Gorse?

EMILY: They certainly do. *(To* PATSY*)* Did Neil go for your father?

PATSY: Yes, Mum.

MRS. HAPGOOD: Then there's young Joe; he's seventeen. And Stevie; he's only eight. We call him the after-thought, eh, Joey?

SHE *roars with laughter, and the* OTHERS *are forced to join in.*

EMILY: Won't you sit down, Mrs. Hapgood.

MRS. HAPGOOD: Oh, "Laurine," please. If we're going to be neighbors, it should be first names, you know.

EMILY: *(Rather uncomfortable, though* MRS. HAPGOOD *is oblivious to the fact)* Yes, indeed. My name is Emily.

MRS. HAPGOOD: Now, that's a nice name.

EMILY: Can I get you some iced tea? Or perhaps you'd like a drink.

HAPGOOD: We don't drink, Mrs. Gorse.

MRS. HAPGOOD: Iced tea would be nice. That's all right, isn't it, Joey?

HAPGOOD: Got caffeine, you know; just as much as coffee.

MRS. HAPGOOD: Oh, a little won't hurt me. I just got to have something cold to drink. *(to* EMILY*)* It's not going to be too much trouble to you now?

EMILY: No trouble at all. It's all ready and waiting in the ice box. How about you, Mr. Hapgood?

HAPGOOD: Plain water for me, please. No ice. Chills the gut.

PATSY: Certainly.

SHE *crosses to the table, where* EMILY *has left water and ice and glasses.*

EMILY: *(As* SHE *pours)* My husband is just coming in now. You'll do the honors, won't you, Pat?

PATSY: Sure, Mum.

EMILY *goes out.* Voices *of the* JUDGE, NEIL, *and* OLIVER *approaching.*

MRS. HAPGOOD: I was just saying to your mother what a beautiful place you got here.

PATSY: We think it's nice, thank you. *(Handing* HAPGOOD *his water)* Here you are, Mr. Hapgood.

HAPGOOD: Thanks...er... Patsy.

MRS. HAPGOOD: It sure is nice. Ever see so many real antiques, Joey? *(A noise at the windows distracts* HER*)* Oh!

The JUDGE *comes in at the window, followed by* NEIL *and* OLIVER.

JUDGE: *(Heartily)* Well, well, well. How are you?

HAPGOOD: *(Shaking hands)* Mr. Gorse? I'm Joe Hapgood.

JUDGE: Yes, indeed.

HAPGOOD: And this is the little woman.

JUDGE: How are you, Mrs. Hapgood. Please don't get up. This is Mr. Purdy. My son-in-law, Mr. Connor. Mrs. Hapgood. Mr. Hapgood.

HE *brings* OLIVER *forward, then* NEIL, *accomplishing the introductions speedily but courteously.* OLIVER *and* NEIL *exchange handshakes and murmured greetings with the* HAPGOODS. *The* JUDGE, *however, barrels on.*

JUDGE: Well! I'm sorry to have kept you waiting; we wandered down to the other end of the field there, and...

MRS. HAPGOOD: Oh, that's all right, Mr. Gorse; Patsy and Emily have been looking after us.

JUDGE: Emi...? Oh. Yes. *(To* PATSY*)* Incidentally, Patsy, what's become of your mother?

PATSY: She's getting the iced tea, Dad.

MRS. HAPGOOD: *(Overlapping* PATSY*)* I was just saying to Joey, I've never seen so many beautiful antiques like you got here, Mr. Gorse.

JUDGE: You're interested in antiques, are you, Mrs. Hapgood?

MRS. HAPGOOD: Oh my, yes! We only have a few things, of course; not like you got. Last week now – I must tell you – I bought this sweetest sort of coffee grinder, you know? Little Joe – he's our boy – seventeen – I was telling Patsy here – well, he's going to make it into a lamp. He's very clever with his hands, young Joe is; takes after his dad. Oh, Joey, tell Mr. Gorse about the highboy. We've got this highboy, you see; it's been in Joey's family for – how many generations is it, Joey?

JUDGE: Really? Not a Chapin, by any chance?

HAPGOOD: What's that?

JUDGE: They were a family of Connecticut furniture makers.

HAPGOOD: I see. Well, I wouldn't know that, Mr. Gorse. But it was made right here in Connecticut, as far as we can tell.

OLIVER: You're of an old Connecticut family, eh, Mr. Hapgood?

HAPGOOD: Oh. yes, Mr....er... Purdy, is it?

OLIVER: That's right: Oliver Purdy.

HAPGOOD: Yes, indeed...er... Oliver, we Hapgoods moved in just about when the Indians moved out.

OLIVER: *(Disconcerted)* Well, I didn't realize that.

EMILY *enters with a pitcher of iced tea and a plate of cookies. During the forgoing,* ALL *have taken seats.* OLIVER *is in an unobtrusive corner,* NEIL *in a straight-backed chair apart from the group. When* EMILY *comes in,* OLIVER, NEIL, HAPGOOD, *and* PATSY *rise.* EMILY *crosses to the table, where* PATSY *joins* HER.

EMILY: Well, here we are.

MRS. HAPGOOD: Mmmm, that looks good!

HAPGOOD: Take it easy now, Mother.

MRS. HAPGOOD: *(Slapping* HIS *hand playfully, then taking it in* HERS) Oh, don't be silly, Joey. *(To the* JUDGE *and* OLIVER) Honestly, he watches me like a hawk. I can't drink this and I can't eat that.

HAPGOOD: Well, you're healthy, ain't you, Mother?

MRS. HAPGOOD: I'm healthy all right. And Joey here, he's got muscles...

EMILY: *(Pouring; to* PATSY) Take this to Mrs. Hapgood, dear; and this one for your father.

MRS. HAPGOOD: You should see him stripped. Show him, Joey.

JUDGE: *(Hastily)* I can well believe it. He doesn't have to...

MRS. HAPGOOD: *(Laughing)* Oh, he's not going to take his clothes off. Just tighten up for Mr. Gorse, Joey.

HAPGOOD *stands and shyly, yet pridefully, tenses his muscles.* NEIL *has moved to the table.*

EMILY: How about you, Neil? Or would you like something...?

MRS. HAPGOOD: Go on, Mr. Gorse, punch him in the stomach.

NEIL: Iced tea will be fine, thank you, Miss Emily.

EMILY *pours for* NEIL. PATSY *hands a glass to* MRS. HAPGOOD. *The* JUDGE *prods* HAPGOOD, *tentatively, in the mid-section.*

MRS. HAPGOOD: *(To* PATSY) Thank you, honey. Well, here's mud in your eye! *(To the* JUDGE) Don't be afraid, Mr. Gorse; you can't hurt him. Hit him hard.

JUDGE: Yes, I can see. That's quite a rock you've got there, isn't it?

HAPGOOD: Same waist measurement when I was twenty-five.

JUDGE: Well, well, well. *(To PATSY, who hands him a glass)* Thank you, dear.

NEIL *has drifted away from the group.* EMILY *pours two more glasses, then crosses over to* OLIVER.

MRS. HAPGOOD: No liquor, no cigarettes, no tea, no coffee. That's the way it is, isn't it, Joey?

HAPGOOD: That's it.

EMILY: *(Offering a glass)* Oliver?

OLIVER: Thank you, Emily; I'll risk it.

JUDGE: I hope he has some vices.

EMILY *silently offers her second glass to* PATSY. HAPGOOD *returns his glass to the table.*

PATSY: You take that one, Mum; I'll get my own.

MRS. HAPGOOD: *(Roguishly)* After all, Mr. Gorse, we have three children.

SHE *goes into gales of laughter. The* JUDGE *joins in, uncomfortably.* EMILY *sits on the sofa beside* MRS. HAPGOOD.

EMILY: Well, this sounds like a merry gathering.

JUDGE: We were...er...talking about Mr. Hapgood's diet. Sounds a bit like Oliver's here.

NEIL *watches* PATSY *pouring, catches her eye.* SHE *begins to smile at him, then turns away.* HAPGOOD *drifts off by himself, surveying the room;* NEIL *joins him.*

MRS. HAPGOOD: Oh? You a health fan, Mr. Purdy?

OLIVER: Not like your husband, Mrs. Hapgood.

HAPGOOD: *(To NEIL)* You the fisherman?

NEIL: Not me; the Judge. I only started yesterday.

OLIVER: I'm concerned about my health. I have to be.

HAPGOOD: Judge?

JUDGE: In Oliver's case, it's rather a matter of locking the barn door after the horse is stolen.

NEIL: That's what they call him. It's a sort of courtesy title.

HAPGOOD: I see.

HAPGOOD *and* NEIL *drift over, associating* THEMSELVES *more with the others.*

MRS. HAPGOOD: You sick then, Mr. Purdy?

HAPGOOD: *(To the JUDGE)* Say, Judge...er...

HE *diverts the* JUDGE'S *attention.*

OLIVER: Well...er...

MRS. HAPGOOD: If you're sick, forget about doctors. They don't know nothing. This is the man you come to. *(SHE indicates HER husband, frustrating HIS attempt to converse with the JUDGE)* Joey's got the gift, you see; haven't you, Joey?

HAPGOOD: What's the trouble, Oliver?

OLIVER: I really don't think...

MRS. HAPGOOD: You tried Yoga? You try that, Yoga and diet, and all your worries are over. Joey, put your foot behind your head for Mr. Purdy.

HAPGOOD: Oh, Mother.

MRS. HAPGOOD: Go on, honey; he'll be interested. You watch this, Mr. Purdy; it's really something.

HAPGOOD: Well, if you're interested...

JUDGE: *(Entering into the spirit; devilishly)* Go ahead, Joe.

HAPGOOD: O.K., then.

JUDGE: Come on, Ollie; get a load of this.

OLIVER *reluctantly rises and comes down beside the* JUDGE. HAPGOOD *sits on the floor, takes hold of one of his feet, lifts it over his head, and locks it behind his ear.* MRS. HAPGOOD *rises and crosses to* HIM.

MRS. HAPGOOD: How about that now?

JUDGE: Well, I'll be! Quite a little tangle you've got there. What do you think of it, Ollie?

HAPGOOD: *(Disengaging his leg)* My wife can do it too. Show them, Mother.

MRS. HAPGOOD: Not just now, Joey.

HAPGOOD: Aw, come on. I did it.

MRS. HAPGOOD: *(Lowering her voice)* Not now, dear.

HAPGOOD: But...

MRS. HAPGOOD: *(stage whisper)* I haven't got my panties on.

EVERYONE *hears this; embarrassed snickers all around, except from* OLIVER, *who takes refuge in* HIS *chair, and the* JUDGE *who laughs outright, unabashedly.* MRS. HAPGOOD *feigns embarrassment, then bursts out laughing* HERSELF.

MRS. HAPGOOD: Gorse, you're a man after my own heart. There's nothing prudish about you. Why, I bet you could take to nudism like a duck to water.

OLIVER: *(Horrified)* Nudism!

MRS. HAPGOOD: *(To the JUDGE)* Just for that I'm going to show you the lotus position. I think I can do it and still be a lady.

JUDGE: In any position, I'm sure you're always a lady.

EMILY, *by now sitting with* PATSY *at the table, is shocked.* SHE *makes a futilely restraining gesture towards* HER *husband.* MRS. HAPGOOD *is sitting on the floor.*

MRS. HAPGOOD: Here we go!

SHE *folds her legs yogi-fashion.*

JUDGE: Well, fancy that!

MRS. HAPGOOD: *(Rocking back and forth)* I could rock on my butt like this all afternoon. *(The* JUDGE *roars with laughter)* Of course, it comes easy to me. I used to be an acrobatic dancer before Joey came along.

JUDGE: *(Helping* HER *up)* I knew it, Mrs. Hapgood; I knew it!

MRS. HAPGOOD: *(Disentangling and rising)* Knew what, Mr. Gorse?

JUDGE: You really *are* Cookie Cuthbert, after all!

MRS. HAPGOOD: *(Bewildered)* Who's she?

JUDGE: *(Lamely; his jest has become awkward)* Oh, a... an old friend of Oliver Purdy's. I was just er...making a joke, that's all.

MRS. HAPGOOD: *(Breaking in on* HIM*)* Why, Oliver! I never would have guessed! Now tell us all about her; confession time, you know!

SHE *flounces over towards the unhappy* OLIVER, *cowering in* HIS *chair. The* JUDGE, *sensing that things are getting out of hand, signals to* EMILY.

EMILY: Mrs. Hapgood. *(Gathering courage)* Laurine.

MRS. HAPGOOD: Yes, honey?

EMILY: Wouldn't you like to see the rest of the house?

MRS. HAPGOOD: Oh, sure. *(To the* OTHERS*)* It's such a beautiful place!

SHE *has forgotten about* OLIVER. EMILY *crosses to* HER, *takes her by the arm, and leads* HER *toward the parlor door.*

EMILY: *(Confidingly)* I think it's time our men-folk got down to business.

MRS. HAPGOOD: You're absolutely right, Emily. I've been gabbing much too much.

EMILY: Not at all dear. *(As* SHE *guides* MRS. HAPGOOD *to the door)* Watch the step now.

MRS. HAPGOOD: Oh, yes. *(Turning at the door)* Talk to them good, Joey.

SHE *goes out, her last remark leaving the* JUDGE *and* OLIVER *distinctly uneasy.*

EMILY: *(At the door)* Coming, Patsy?

PATSY: Sure, Mum.

EMILY *goes out,* PATSY *following. The* JUDGE *crosses up toward the door.*

EMILY'S VOICE: Afterwards we can take a look at the garden.

MRS. HAPGOOD'S VOICE: Oh that'll be nice.

The JUDGE *closes the door. There is a second's pause for* HIM *to collect* HIMSELF.

JUDGE: Your wife is certainly a live wire, Mr. Hapgood.

HAPGOOD: *(Good naturedly)* She means all right, Judge. She's a good scout.

JUDGE: *(Sincerely)* I can see that.

HAPGOOD: She loves life, you see, every minute of it.

JUDGE: *(Very sincerely)* I do too, Joe; I do too. Now, suppose you sit here. *(HE indicates the sofa)* And, Neil, park yourself there. All right? *(NEIL takes the seat indicated, one of the easy chairs.* HAPGOOD *sits on the sofa. To* HAPGOOD*)* You're sure you won't have a drink? Glass of water perhaps? *(*HAPGOOD *holds up his hand, indicating "No")* Well, then...

HE *is uneasy, uncertain how to begin.*

HAPGOOD: Neil here tells me you're quite a fisherman.

JUDGE: Well...

NEIL: I said he fished. As a matter of fact, Mr. Hapgood, he is quite a fisherman.

JUDGE: *(diffidently)* Well, it's a blameless pastime.

HAPGOOD: You can say that again.

JUDGE: *(warming)* You like to fish, Joe?

HAPGOOD: I sure do. Been at it since I was knee high to a hop-toad. Tell me, Judge, do you use this new spinner contraption.

JUDGE: Oh, I've got one, but I never seem to make it work right. I guess you just can't teach an old dog new tricks, and I'm getting to be a pretty old dog now.

HAPGOOD: I know how it is. Like I always say, the old ways are the best. Give me a good old-fashioned casting rod any time.

OLIVER: *(Testing* HAPGOOD*)* Do you ever work with a plug?

HAPGOOD: Plug's all right for pickerel, I guess. But I think the real sporting fish around these parts is your little old bass, don't you think so?

OLIVER: *(Guardedly)* Yes; I er...agree with you.

HE *regards* HAPGOOD *suspiciously.* NEIL *picks up the flagging conversation.*

NEIL: *(With unusual enthusiasm)* The Judge took me over to Deacon's Pond yesterday. I understand that's one of the best bass spots in the whole state.

HAPGOOD: That's what I've always heard.

JUDGE: Well, it's not what it was when I was a youngster, I can tell you that.

NEIL: It's good enough for me. I think it's a beautiful place.

JUDGE: *(Looking* NEIL *straight in the eye, quietly)* Do you really think so, Neil?

NEIL: *(Meeting the* JUDGE'S *gaze)* Yes. I do.

The JUDGE *grins.* HE *has the encouragement* HE *has been looking for, and* HE *takes the bit now in his teeth.*

JUDGE: You know, Mr. Hapgood, we have a zoning law here that applies...

HAPGOOD: I know all about it, Judge. I figured that was what you wanted to talk to me about.

JUDGE: *(Quite disarmed)* Well, I...er... Mr. Purdy and I thought that if you were planning to build an amusement park there...

HAPGOOD: *(Exploding)* Amusement park! Honestly, Judge, where did you ever get that idea?

JUDGE: I thought...er...well, after all, Happylands Amusement Park, isn't that...?

HAPGOOD: Oh, no, no, no. That sort of thing's all right for Wethersford, but you're not going to get people to drive thirty miles into the sticks just to ride a Ferris wheel. You know, I kind of suspected you must have had some misconception of what I had in mind. But an amusement park: never!

JUDGE: I'm mighty happy to hear that, let me tell you.

HAPGOOD: Of course, of course. Now, even though your zoning law doesn't specifically list such parks among its restrictions, well, I've studied it pretty carefully – as I always do when I'm buying a piece of property anywhere – and I'm pretty sure that, if you or anyone wanted to fight the idea, that law could be interpreted in such a way as to give you all the support you'd ever need. But that's beside the point. As I said, in the first place, it would be a pretty darned impractical proposition – from a commercial point of view, that is. And, in the second place, I'm not the sort of guy that goes around messing up nature where nature hasn't been pretty much messed up already.

JUDGE: I am glad to hear that, Joe. I think I've brought you out here on a false alarm.

OLIVER, *too, is visibly relieved. Mopping* HIS *brow,* HE *crosses to the table, pours* HIMSELF *a glass of iced tea, and sits there, nursing such lingering doubts as* HE *might have to* HIMSELF. HAPGOOD *rises and shakes hands with the* JUDGE.

HAPGOOD: It's been a pleasure, sir, believe me. I hope we'll get to see a lot of each other from now on.

NEIL: Mr. Hapgood, you haven't told us what you *are* planning to do up on the lake there.

HAPGOOD: Oh, I haven't, have I? Well, listen to this, Judge. I think it's a great little idea, if I do say so myself.

JUDGE: *(Sitting on the chair, U.R., vacated by* OLIVER*)* What is it, Joe?

HAPGOOD: Well, I've always thought, you see, it was sort of a shame that so many people who live and work in towns like Wethersford and Middleburg and Grafton, they get their two weeks vacation every summer and where do they go? New York? Who wants to go to a big city in the middle of summer? Maine, perhaps, or New Hampshire? That's more like it. But you waste a couple of days getting there and back, and you're all pooped out from driving. Why spend the time and the money, I said to myself, when, only an hour or an hour and a half away, you've got a place like Deacon's Pond here. There you can relax, swim a little, boat a little, catch yourself a fish, forget about the Russians, and get back home all rested up and still have a little money left in your pocket. You see what I mean?

JUDGE: *(With misgivings)* Yes, I do.

OLIVER *glowers darkly.*

HAPGOOD: Now, I'm not talking about anything fancy, you see. People who want that, well, they can afford to go someplace else. What I'm talking about is…well, more like a camp, see? They have camps for kids; why not have camps for grown-ups, too?

JUDGE: Why not?

HAPGOOD: For example, there are these places in the Catskills; they've got regular nightclubs there – my wife used to work them – just like New York City or Miami Beach. But who needs a whole orchestra and specialty acts and that sort of thing out in the country? Why, all you have to do is build a platform, put up some Japanese lanterns, plug in the old record player, and there's as good a dancehall as you'd ever want to see.

JUDGE: Uh-huh.

OLIVER, *quite upset, rises and begins to pace nervously.*

HAPGOOD: Simple. Get it? People like to entertain themselves. We'd have an entertainment director, of course, and he could sort of get up amateur acts, you know, and community sings, stuff like that. And then I've got an "in" with this dealer, you see, who can get me a couple of motor boats for about half what you'd have to pay for them. *(OLIVER, appalled, stops dead in HIS tracks)* I wouldn't let the campers run them by themselves, of course, but my son…

OLIVER: Motor boats, did you say, Mr. Hapgood?

HAPGOOD: *(Turning in his seat; cheerfully)* Oh, people love 'em, Mr. Purdy. I could do without them for myself, you understand, but…well, this is the age of speed, and…

OLIVER: *(Beginning to splutter)* But…but…

The JUDGE *rises, waves* OLIVER *to his seat by the table and addresses* HAPGOOD.

JUDGE: Now look here, Joe. I think I get the picture pretty clearly.

HAPGOOD: It's a good idea, don't you think so, Judge?

JUDGE: Well, yes, Joe, it is. And I must say I appreciate your concern for the recreational needs of the people of Wethereford and other municipalities in that area; but…

HAPGOOD: Don't go overboard, Judge; I happen to think it's a sound financial proposition as well.

JUDGE: *(Dryly)* I didn't imagine that you had entirely overlooked that aspect of the matter. What I wanted to say, however, was that Deacon's Pond is not, in my humble opinion, perhaps quite the place for an establishment of the kind you speak of.

HAPGOOD: I can get the property for a fair price; there's a good, all-weather road into there from the other side of – what do they call it? – Copp's Hill; and–

JUDGE: *(Impatiently)* Yes; yes.

HAPGOOD: *(Plowing on)* The water supply is more than adequate – spring house and an artesian well; the tax rate is favorable; the...

JUDGE: I didn't mean that, Joe. I'm sure that the Winfield property has all the advantages you mention. But don't you think this camp of yours would somewhat, let us say, disturb the peculiar quality, the virtue of our little lake here?

HAPGOOD: No, I don't really; I–

JUDGE: *(Over-riding* HIM; *gaining momentum)* After all, what is it we especially like about Deacon's Pond? You're a fisherman, Joe; I should think you'd be one of the first to recognize it.

HAPGOOD: I... I...

JUDGE: Isn't it the peace, the calm, the solitude of the place? A man out on that lake is in communion with nature – with God, if you like – in the simplest and most direct sort of way. He is reminded there of his primordial partnership in the whole big, blinking universe. I think that's pretty important, Joe, in this harum-scarum, here-today-gone-tomorrow world of ours: to know that somewhere you belong, you fit in.

HAPGOOD: I'm sure of that, Judge, but–

JUDGE: And how the hell can you commune with dance halls and Japanese lanterns? *(Chidingly)* And motor boats, Joe?

HAPGOOD: Well, I...

JUDGE: As a fisherman, you should know that the exhaust fumes from these boats would kill just about every fish in the lake in one season, not to speak of the noise and the churning up of the water and all. I have a couple of friends on the State Fish and Game Commission, and they're particularly interested in Deacon's Pond – as conservationists, that is. Now, if I should bring this motor boat business to their attention, I'm pretty sure they'd...

NEIL, *disturbed, rises, crosses to the cupboard, L., gets the pitcher, takes it to the table – skirting* OLIVER, *who at the moment is looking rather pleased with himself – and pours himself an iced tea.*

HAPGOOD: Now about those motor boats, Judge–

JUDGE: *(Ignoring* HIM*)* Then the good people of our town meeting, they're a pretty old-fashioned bunch, I guess you'd say. I don't mean to imply that they wholly disapprove of dancing and community singing and the like. They're not exactly medieval. But they can be pretty uppity about... well, I suppose it would come under the heading of "disturbing the peace". There are a couple of families that have homes on the lake – they're rather unobtrusive buildings; you'd hardly know they were there – and these are, happily, very quiet people. They go to bed early, and they keep pretty much to themselves. Well, if it were pointed out that–

HAPGOOD: *(Still courteous, but with an unexpected edge to* HIS *voice)* Just a minute, Mr. Gorse. You don't have to go any further; I know just what you're driving at.

JUDGE: *(Backing down just a little)* I didn't want to threaten you, Joe.

HAPGOOD: I could see that. You were dancing around there sort of. You didn't want to threaten me; but you were threatening me just the same.

JUDGE: *(Sheepishly)* Well…

HAPGOOD: I dare say you swing quite a bit of influence around this town, Judge.

JUDGE: I think I'm held in…uh…some esteem in these parts. I don't know if I deserve it, but…

HAPGOOD: I'm sure you deserve it. You have my respect anyway.

JUDGE: *(Dismissing the compliment with a gesture)* I believe I could exert some pressure. I rarely have. I don't really want to.

HAPGOOD: I'm sure you don't want to. But you could and you would if it was necessary.

JUDGE: *(Regarding* HIM *evenly)* You're quite right, Joe.

HAPGOOD: Of course. I'm the same way myself: a peaceful man at heart; but I'll fight if I'm cornered. Now, I don't know just what the odds are here. You could hold me up for quite a while, I suppose; you might even be able to beat me out in the end. But I'll give you quite a run for your money, Judge; and, if I don't win, one of these days somebody like me will.

JUDGE: You think so?

HAPGOOD: It stands to reason, Judge. You can't hog that lake for yourself and your friend Purdy here forever.

OLIVER, *becoming tense again, slams down* HIS *glass.*

JUDGE: *(*HIS *dander up)* Look here, Mr. Hapgood, there has never been any question of my trying to appropriate that lake to myself. The shores…

HAPGOOD: *(Turning in* HIS *seat)* Does that go for you, too, Mr. Purdy?

OLIVER *rises. The* JUDGE *makes a pacifying gesture that prevents his speaking.* OLIVER *begins to pace, nervous and fretful.*

JUDGE: I was saying: the shores of that lake are private property, but the lake itself is open to the public, and there's a road into it that anyone can use. It is not within my power to close that road, and there is no question of my asking for such a power.

HAPGOOD: But the facilities for the public on Deacon's Pond are limited are they not?

JUDGE: They are indeed. But I'm one of several individuals that keep a boat on the pond, and I'm willing to take out just about anyone who asks to come along with me. Friend or stranger. I've done it many times.

HAPGOOD: Are you willing to take out every day twenty or thirty lathe-turners and shoe clerks from Wethersford or Middleburg?

JUDGE: Well, there's a limit to my boat's capacity, of course; but I've never drawn the line at a lathe-turner or a shoe clerk or anybody else. Just so long as they're interested in–

HAPGOOD: Just so long as they want to "commune with nature" your way. Isn't that about the size of it, Judge?

JUDGE: *(Off balance)* Well, er... *(Suddenly vehement)* What the hell's wrong with my way?

HAPGOOD: Nothing. For *you*. I like your way myself.

JUDGE: Well, then?

HAPGOOD: But what's it going to mean to a guy who's been sweating behind a bench all his life? He's probably not an expert fisherman. He's not about to spend two hours by himself in a boat perfecting his cast. You and I were born with fish-poles in our hands: it's different with us. But all he wants to do is throw a plug around for half an hour and say he's been fishing. And then, maybe, he'd like to take a swim or have a boat ride. And in the evening, he wants to dance with his wife or play a game of hearts, drink some beer and, maybe, sing a few songs. What's wrong with that, will you tell me? Isn't he communing with nature, too? He's breathing fresh air for a change. He's got the woods all around him and the stars at night overhead.

JUDGE: I...uh... *(Pleading)* Neil, you were out with me yesterday. You know what I mean, don't you?

NEIL: Yes, I do.

JUDGE: *(Hopefully)* And you agree with me, don't you, Neil?

NEIL: *(After a long pause; very softly)* I agree...with Mr. Hapgood, Judge.

JUDGE: *(At a loss for words)* Oh.

Seeing the JUDGE *flounder and unable further to contain himself,* OLIVER *advances.*

OLIVER: Calvin Gorse, what's come over you? Have you no mind of your own that you have to ask this little commie whippersnapper's opinion?

JUDGE: Now, hold on, Ollie...

OLIVER: I'm sorry, Cal, but I can't sit by any longer and watch you back down.

JUDGE: *(Raising* His *voice)* I haven't backed down, Ollie.

OLIVER: Well, I don't know what you're doing then. Don't you realize that everything you value in life is at stake? I'm surprised at you, Cal. I thought you were going to stand up for me and...

JUDGE: I am standing up for you. I only...

OLIVER: *(Topping* HIM) Then why the hell don't you stop pussy-footing around with this man? First thing you know, you're going to open up the lake to every stumblebum in Wethersford just because this cheap little faker and his hootchie-cootchie girl-friend have...

JUDGE: *(At the top of* His *voice)* Oliver!

OLIVER *is shocked into silence.* HAPGOOD *has sat patiently through the blast, his head lowered.* NEIL *is at the window. There is a pause.*

JUDGE: *(Very gently)* I think you'd better leave, Ollie.

OLIVER: Yes, Cal. *(HE starts to go, but stops at the window)* Cal?

JUDGE: *(Ignoring OLIVER; very calmly, though faltering)* Mr. Hapgood, I… uh… wish you the very best of luck in your venture. I think your…er… campers will have reason to be most grateful to you, because there just isn't a lovelier place in the whole world than Deacon's Pond.

HE *looks at* OLIVER *standing at the window.* THEY *stare at each other a long moment; then* OLIVER *goes out. The* JUDGE *turns upstage, takes out a handkerchief and blows* HIS *nose furiously.*

JUDGE: *(With forced gaiety, keeping his back to* HAPGOOD*)* Well, I'd better round up the ladies, eh Joe?

HE *starts for the parlor door.*

NEIL: *(At the window, looking out)* They're out here, Judge.

JUDGE: *(Changing direction and heading for the window)* Right.

NEIL: Shall I get them?

JUDGE: No, Neil; I'll go.

HE *is at the window at this point.* HE *pats* NEIL *on the shoulder, gives* HIM *an affectionate squeeze, and goes out.* HAPGOOD *has risen.*

HAPGOOD: *(After a pause)* He was crying, wasn't he?

NEIL: He'll be all right in a moment.

HAPGOOD: An amazing man.

NEIL: You can say that again.

HAPGOOD: Hmm.

NEIL: *(Coming downstage)* There's just one thing, Mr. Hapgood.

HAPGOOD: Joe. Please.

NEIL: Joe.

HAPGOOD: What is it, Neil?

NEIL: About those motor boats. The lake, you know, isn't all that big. It's pretty shallow in spots, and there's apt to be logs and stumps and things just below the surface of the water. They make good places for the fish to hole up in, but I think they might raise hob with a motor boat.

HAPGOOD: You may be right, Neil. It was just that I could get them at a bargain.

NEIL: I know, but I just don't think it's a very practical idea for that particular pond. And they're not really handy to fish from, are they?

HAPGOOD: Well, perhaps not.

NEIL: And I imagine, as the Judge says, they do give off fumes and…

HAPGOOD: Say no more, Neil. We'll forget about the motor boats.

NEIL: The Judge will be happy.

HAPGOOD: My pleasure.

The JUDGE, EMILY, PATSY, *and* MRS. HAPGOOD *arrive at the window. The* JUDGE *has completely regained his equilibrium.* HE *stands aside in an attitude of exaggerated gallantry to let the ladies pass in before* HIM. MRS. HAPGOOD, *as* SHE *enters, interrupts her prattling with* EMILY *to acknowledge his gesture with an equally elaborate curtsy followed by a little giggle.*

MRS. HAPGOOD: It's just the most beautiful place I've ever seen. I should think you and your husband would just be so happy here you'd never want to go anywheres. *(Curtsy)* Oh, Joey, you should see Emily's garden! It's just the most beautiful thing in the world. She's got everything growing there. *(Turning back to* EMILY*)* You sure got a green thumb, honey. That's all I can say: you got a green thumb.

EMILY: I don't know about the green thumb, but, after I've been working in it a while, I can vouch for a very stiff back.

MRS. HAPGOOD: *(A laugh; then coyly)* Yoga, my dear. Yoga's the answer. *(Crossing down to her husband, lowering her voice)* Everything settled, Joey?

HAPGOOD: Everything's fine, Mother.

The JUDGE *and* EMILY *come down.* PATSY *and* NEIL *are left up by the window. There is still some distance between* THEM; THEY *try not to look at each other, but it isn't easy.*

JUDGE: Yes, we're looking forward to your being neighbors of ours.

EMILY *takes his hand in hers and gives it a reassuring squeeze.*

EMILY: How about some more iced tea? We'll celebrate. Water for you, Mr. Hapgood?

HAPGOOD: *(Looking at* HIS *watch)* We'd better get a move on, Mother. I'm sorry, Emily; but I didn't realize it was so late. We've got to go.

EMILY: Oh, must you?

MRS. HAPGOOD: If Joey says we must, we must. But I could stay here forever.

EMILY: Well, you'll be coming this way again soon I hope.

MRS. HAPGOOD: I sure hope so, Emily.

JUDGE: Perhaps you'd like to take a turn on the lake with me one of these days, Joe. You're not going to have much time for fishing when you start working on that camp.

HAPGOOD: You're right about that, Judge. I'd sure like to get in all I can before the crowd hits me.

JUDGE: Just call me anytime.

HAPGOOD: I sure appreciate that.

MRS. HAPGOOD: *(At the door with* EMILY*)* Come on, Joey; you're the one who said it was late.

HAPGOOD: You go ahead, Mother; I just want to tell the Judge something.

MRS. HAPGOOD: *(Softly to* EMILY*)* Men! They've got more secrets than we'll ever know.

EMILY: *(With a little laugh)* I'll come along with you.

MRS. HAPGOOD: *(Waving)* G'bye, Patsy. Neil.

PATSY: Good-bye, Mrs. Hapgood   NEIL: Good-bye.

> MRS. HAPGOOD *goes out.* EMILY, *following* HER, *turns at the doorway and blows a kiss to the* JUDGE, *which* HE *acknowledges with a wink.* SHE *goes out.*

HAPGOOD: No secret really, Judge; I just wanted to tell you that I'm calling off the motor boats.

JUDGE: Oh, I am glad to hear that, Joe.

HAPGOOD: Yeah. You can thank Neil here for it. He talked me out of the idea.

JUDGE: *(Turning toward* NEIL*)* Well, I'll be...

> HE *is a bit dazed and quite pleased.* PATSY, *upstage of* NEIL, *regards* HER *husband admiringly.* NEIL *affects diffidence.*

HAPGOOD: Be seeing you, Judge.

JUDGE: *(Turning, but not fully attentive to* HAPGOOD'S *departure)* Oh, yes. Good-bye, Joe.

HAPGOOD: *(Shaking the* JUDGE'S *hand)* Good-bye, and thank you for everything,

JUDGE: *(Still somewhat bewildered)* Not at all.

> HAPGOOD *moves swiftly to the door and salutes* PATSY *and* NEIL *before leaving.*

HAPGOOD: So long, kids.

PATSY: Good-bye.   NEIL: 'Bye, Joe.

> HAPGOOD *goes out. The* JUDGE *collects* HIS *wits and goes to the door.*

JUDGE: Joe... (HE *decides there is no need to follow him, turns back into the room and comes downstage, meeting* NEIL*)* I do want to thank you, Neil, for speaking about those boats to Mr. Hapgood.

NEIL: It should have been obvious to him they wouldn't fit in. Eventually, I think, he'd have come to the same decision on his own.

JUDGE: All the same, I appreciate it, my boy. (HE *pats* NEIL *on the shoulder in a spirit of affectionate camaraderie)* Look, Neil, can't you stay a day or two longer? You could have another crack at that bass you missed.

NEIL: Well, I...

PATSY: *(Coming to* NEIL'S *rescue; gently, but firmly)* We ought to be going just about now. I'm sorry, Pop, but Neil's a working man.

JUDGE: But, why not...?

PATSY: *(Gently, but more firmly)* And we've a lot of things to do when we get home.

> NEIL *puts his arm about* HER. SHE *offers no resistance.*

JUDGE: Whatever you say.

HE *feels rather like an intruder; embarrassed,* HE *moves away, pretending to examine the books on the shelves.*

PATSY: I'd better pack our bags.

NEIL: I'll give you a hand,

PATSY: No; you keep Pop company for a while. I'll call you when I need you. (SHE *gives* HIM *a peck on the cheek. Very softly)* Darling.

NEIL *kisses* HER. THEY *continue to embrace until the* JUDGE, *turning and seeing* THEM, *coughs pointedly and turns away again.* NEIL *releases* HER, *and* PATSY *crosses to the parlor door.*

JUDGE: *(Stopping* PATSY *at the door)* You know something, Mrs. Connor, I like this husband of yours.

PATSY: I rather like him myself. And do you know something, Mr. Gorse?

JUDGE: What's that?

PATSY: I never heard you say "Mrs. Connor" before.

JUDGE: Well, that's who you are, aren't you?

PATSY: *(Softly)* That's who I am.

SHE *goes.*

JUDGE: Well, well, well!

NEIL: *(Mischievously)* Well, well yourself, Judge.

JUDGE: *(Turning)* What do you mean by that?

NEIL: I think I've got a convert on my hands.

JUDGE: The hell you have, my boy. I did what I did because Oliver forced my hand. If he hadn't... *(Stopping short; remembering)* Hey, wait a minute! I never apologized to Joe.

NEIL: He didn't ask for an apology.

JUDGE: All the same... *(Abandoning the idea, returning to his earlier line of thought)* Well, anyway, as I was saying, after Ollie's little outburst, if I had acted in any other way, I should have been acting as something other than a gentleman.

NEIL: *(Teasing)* I'm disappointed in you, Judge. I thought you'd suddenly become a liberal.

JUDGE: *(Playing the curmudgeon)* Ach, you fellows are all alike. Every half-way decent action you want to stick your label on. Do you really think you've got a monopoly on kindness, consideration, and respect for your fellow man? Let me tell you, boy, there are and always have been rascals on both sides of the fence; and men of good will, too. *(More gently)* Seriously, Neil, the thought occurred to me: one of these days, one of those "stumblebums," as Ollie calls them, may just happen to find himself alone in a boat in the north bay of Deacon's Pond. And it just could be that, in the quiet there, with only the sound of the peepers singing and maybe a big fat bass plopping out of the water to catch a May-fly and perhaps a wood-duck calling overhead, it just could be that, for a little while, he'll find no need for the distractions of the crowd. Mind you, Neil, I have no grouse about card games and community sings – only when they represent a terrified flight from the larger identification. That's what I hope our stumblebum will discover: just when he thinks he is most alone, that he is never alone. He is a partner to every blade of grass, to every water drop, to every star; that is his glorious security. And all the fields and forests, all the oceans, and all the galaxies are within him; that is his glorious responsibility. *(He pauses a second; then, more brightly)* Well, we'll never get him to that state unless we lure him out to the lake there somehow. And it could be Hapgood's Japanese lanterns are just the thing to turn the trick.

NEIL: Could be.

JUDGE: Well, Oliver should be home by now. I'd better give him a call and see if he wants to go out on the lake tomorrow.

NEIL: I don't get it. After the way he behaved here this afternoon, you're going to make up to him just like that.

JUDGE: Well, I wasn't thinking exactly of "making up to him." I figure the less said about it, the better.

NEIL: And you'll just go off fishing as if nothing had happened?

JUDGE: *(Amazed at NEIL's amazement)* Oliver is my friend, Neil. You don't chuck thirty years of friendship in one afternoon.

NEIL: I know, but after...

JUDGE: Neil, when the sun goes down behind Copp's Hill, and the light on Deacon's Pond turns silver, and the Piper calls, "Come home, come home," Ollie hears him too.

The JUDGE goes into the parlor to telephone.

CURTAIN

THE MAN IN THE TWEED SUIT

a one act play

The Man in the Tweed Suit

In 1982, The Polaris Repertory Company presented a reading before an audience of *The Man in the Tweed Suit*, along with *The Edge of the Abyss* and a third short play, *For Richer, For Poorer* by the same writer. The play was performed in 1995 at Polaris North, a successor organization, with two other one-acts by other playwrights. This production was directed by William-Kevin Young with Duff Dugan, Victoria Thompson, and Tom Williams appearing in the cast and Danna Call and Steven Packard as radio voices.

cast

A Man

His Wife

A Caller

Radio Voices

setting

The living room-dining room of a cottage of efficient modern design. Stage right: a door leading out. Left: a sideboard; upon it, a radio; above it, a wall cabinet. To the left of center stage: a dining table with two chairs. Across the upstage wall: a wide inset fitted with a comfortably cushioned window seat beneath a large, single-paned picture window.

Black and white. There is no other color, nor any intermediate tones of gray. White predominates, black serving only to outline the forms of the various objects within the room. Beyond the window there is a lunar landscape, white mountains against a black sky, where glows a solitary crescent of light, just above the mountain rim. White and black.

Music is heard before the curtain rises, a simple nodal strain played upon stringed instruments. This emanates, as we soon see, from the radio; a MAN *is listening to it, a* WOMAN *seated beside him on the window seat.* THEY *too are entirely in black and white, and their hair is black, as are their lips and eyes. Listening to the music, they seem almost to be asleep; perhaps they are.* HIS *head is tipped back, and* HERS *rests upon his shoulder.* THEY *sit very close to each other; her hand is lightly held in his.*

The music soon ends. It is followed by the distant ringing of a dinner bell and the VOICE OF AN ANNOUNCER *in the distance, calling, "Dinner time!" The bell is rung again, closer to the microphone, and the announcer more loudly repeats his information: "Dinner time!"* HIS *voice fades away with a final, far-off ringing of the bell. The* MAN *on the window seat has stirred meanwhile and straightened. As if automatically, at the mention of dinner,* HE *passes his hand tentatively across his stomach. Now* HE *is looking at his* WIFE, *who has also roused herself, and seems on the verge of speaking; but a* VOICE *over the radio speaks in his stead:*

RADIO MAN'S VOICE: My, I'm hungry! What's for dinner tonight?

The MAN *in white does not seem surprised, even though, as we shall discover when* HE *speaks, the voice* HE *has heard is his own.* HE *smiles at his wife as if in acknowledgment that the radio voice has exactly expressed his thoughts. Her radio counterpart replies:*

RADIO WOMAN'S VOICE: Whatever would please you. What would you like?

RADIO MAN'S VOICE: Well, uh...let me see...

HE *shrugs his shoulders as a sign of his indifference.*

RADIO ANNOUNCER: Haven't an idea? How about a tip from the Master Chef? When it comes to planning a meal, he's always good for a good suggestion.

Very effusively.

And here he is now! The Master Chef!

RADIO MASTER CHEF: *(His voice, cultured, mellifluous, almost hypnotic)* Good evening. May I suggest you try tonight a dish at once nourishing, agreeable to the taste, and requiring literally no preparation. There is a fruit which you can readily identify by the singular pattern of its star-shaped markings. This you will find growing upon a vine at the end of your garden, not fifty paces from your door. The leaves of the vine, incidentally, may be served as a delicious salad. The fruit is large, and one will make for each person an entirely satisfying repast. All you have to do is slice it and eat. Cooking it is quite unnecessary; it would, in fact, impair its remarkable nutritive values, which it has in full abundance, containing all the vitamins, minerals, fats, proteins, and carbohydrates needed to sustain you in perfect health until your morning meal.

RADIO MAN'S VOICE: Say, that's what I'd like!

RADIO WOMAN'S VOICE: That's for me too!

RADIO MAN'S VOICE: I'll go and pick dinner then.

RADIO WOMAN'S VOICE: And I'll set the table.

RADIO ANNOUNCER: And thank you for your very helpful suggestion, Master Chef!

Again the sound of the dinner bell and the ANNOUNCER'S VOICE, *fading, calling, "Dinner time!" The music comes up, the same melody as before. During the preceding interchange, the* MAN *and his* WIFE *have continued to suit their actions to the voices of their counterparts on the air.* THEY *have risen;* HE *has gone toward the door, and* SHE *has moved toward the cupboard above the sideboard, left. At the door* HE *stops and turns to his* WIFE, *who turns toward him.*

MAN: Easy enough, isn't it?

WIFE: Blessedly easy.

RADIO MASTER CHEF: *(Voice over the music)* And there is nothing you want?

MAN: *(Like a child, reciting a lesson leaned by rote)* I want nothing save that by which, by wanting it I am satisfied. Want to me describes only the moment when I say, "I want." I have scarcely time to speak the words, even to think of them, before my want is gone. I have my house for shelter, food and fresh water forever at my door; when I am weary, my bed is ready to receive me, and sleep comes easily. My ears are filled with music; my eyes, with the picture of all pleasure. And my wife is always beside me to give me all companionship and love.

WIFE: I want only a tomorrow as joyful as yesterday.

RADIO MASTER CHEF: And you remember nothing?

WIFE: I remember nothing save that yesterday was as joyful as today.

To her husband.

Why does he always ask that?

MAN: Damned if I know.

RADIO MASTER CHEF: Quite right, young man. You understand that, if you so desire, you are always able to return.

MAN: Return where?   WIFE: Where to?

A little laugh acknowledges their unanimity.

WIFE: There: he's said that again too. Why?

MAN: Search me. Some little joke of his, I guess. I don't always appreciate his sense of humor.

WIFE: Where have we ever been but here?

MAN: Nowhere that I know of.

WIFE: No; never anywhere else but here.

A pause: HE *turns to go.*

And yet...

MAN: *(Turning back)* Yes?

WIFE: At times, at night, when you're asleep and I don't feel like sleeping, I get out of bed and sit for a while by the window. Perhaps the Earth is full, and I will sit and watch its great, round light hung above the mountain. Sometimes then, I have the strangest – I cannot quite describe it – feeling. Here.

SHE *presses her left hand to her side. At the same moment the music coming over the radio is interrupted by a crackling of static, brief but violent.* SHE *turns to it in some alarm.*

WIFE: That never happened before. Maybe we should call the Chief Electrician.

MAN: You never told me this before. Maybe we should call the Surgeon General.

WIFE: Why?

MAN: Perhaps there is something he could do for you. Give you a pill or something.

WIFE: Whatever for?

MAN: You just said…

WIFE: Said? What did I say?

MAN: (*Seeing she has quite forgotten*) Oh, nothing. Nothing at all.

WIFE: (*Close to him, pleading playfully*) Tell me.

HE *chuckles affectionately and puts his arms about her.* SHE, *laughing, returns his embrace.*

WIFE: Oh, you! You're teasing me!

MAN: When did our happiness begin, a minute or a million years ago? I have lost count of time since there has been no day different from the rest to mark the beginning of my memory.

WIFE: Would you ever want such a day?

MAN: Not on your life! To be different, it would have to be less than perfect.

WIFE: Then may all our days be perfect days.

MAN: I think they will be; don't you?

WIFE: I hope so.

Breaking from him.

Now, run along and get that…

MAN: (*Imitating the* MASTER CHEF *with exaggerated pomposity*) …"fruit which you can readily identify by the singular pattern of its star-shaped markings."

Opening the door.

We'll have to think of a name for it.

WIFE: How about just "star-fruit"?

MAN: I suppose that will do: not very imaginative, but accurate, to the point, and easy enough to say; in fact, practical as a housewife and altogether obvious.

WIFE: (*Playfully pushing him out*) Oh, get out, you clown!

SHE *closes the door after him and turns away, starting to cross left.* SHE *is stopped by his reopening the door, putting in his head, blowing her a kiss, and retreating again, closing the door behind him.*

WIFE: (*Shaking her head and smiling after him*) Such a baby!

HER *smile fades into melancholy.* Suddenly SHE *winces, holding her left side as though* SHE *felt a stitch there. The radio responds with a spasm of static; then her pain has evidently gone, and the music is resumed. Cheerful again, humming to the music,* SHE *goes about setting the table. From the cabinet, left,* SHE *takes and arranges a pitcher of water, two tumblers, two knives, and two plates.* SHE *has just set down one plate and is holding the other in her hand when there is a knock at the door.*

WIFE: (*Running to the door*) Well it certainly didn't take you long!

SHE *throws open the door and steps back with a little shriek of surprise, dropping her plate, which shatters on the floor. In the doorway is a gentleman dressed in a tweed suit, with matching cap and well-made walking shoes.* HIS *shirt is of red and green plaid, and his tie is green.* HE *sports a cane, a rose in his lapel buttonhole, a brave orange-red moustache, and an elegantly trimmed beard of the same impressive hue.* HE *doffs his cap grandly, revealing a fine crop of reddish hair.*

THE CALLER: (*Bowing*) Allow me, madam.

HE *stoops to pick up the pieces of the broken plate as* SHE *stands by, dumbfounded, staring at him.* HE *straightens up and hands her the pieces, which* SHE *takes rather as though* SHE *were in a trance. The words, "Thank you," are on her lips, but* SHE *can find no voice for them.*

CALLER: I must apologize for frightening you.

WIFE: (*Collecting herself*) No; not at all. It's just that I didn't expect... I thought it would be my husband.

CALLER: (*Coming into the room*) I saw him just now in the garden, but he didn't see me. He was picking star-fruit leaves for a salad.

WIFE: Star-fruit! Funny that you should call it that, too. We just named it.

CALLER: Really? I thought you always called it that.

WIFE: Always?

CALLER: I mean to say... well, it's rather the obvious name for it; isn't it now?

WIFE: (*Pouting a little as* SHE *puts the broken plate on the table*) I suppose so. That's what my husband said anyway.

CALLER: (*Tactfully*) Never mind; I think it's a very nice name.

SHE *smiles at him appreciatively.* HE *is staring into her eyes with an amused expression, as if waiting for recognition, which doesn't come.*

CALLER: Then you don't remember me at all, do you?

WIFE: I'm very sorry. Should I?

CALLER: No; I don't suppose you should, what with one thing or another. Besides, we were a good deal younger then, and I didn't have this.

Indicating his beard.

WIFE: Then? When? Have you ever been here before?

CALLER: No, not here.

Amiably, after a pause.

I've been meaning to call on you for a long while, but frankly I've been so hellishly busy working on my own place I haven't had time to realize I was lonely. Now that I've done about all I can do with it, I find myself with nothing to occupy me and a terrible yearning for company.

WIFE: (*Pleasantly, but* HER *awkwardness betrays her inexperience as a hostess*) You're very welcome here. Won't you?

Indicating a chair, right of the table.

CALLER: (*Sitting*) Thanks.

Taking out and glancing at his watch, with a whistle of surprise.

Whew! I've been a time getting here! Already I'll have to start thinking about going back.

WIFE: (*Disappointed*) Oh, what a shame! But you can stay a little while, can't you?

CALLER: Only a moment.

WIFE: Well, I'm glad for that at least. We never have any callers, except the Governor, of course.

Casting about for a gesture of hospitality; taking up the water pitcher.

Can I offer you something to drink?

CALLER: What's that? Water?

WIFE: (*As though saying, "Of course"*) Yes.

CALLER: No, thank you; I never touch it.

WIFE: But it's...

CALLER: I know; fresh from your garden fountain and full of all the vitamins, minerals, fats, proteins, and carbohydrates required to sustain you in perfect health till Kingdom Come. Do you mind if I smoke?

WIFE: Wha...? I mean: no.

HE *has taken out a gold cigarette case;* SHE *retreats a step, perplexed and timorous.*

CALLER: (*Offering her a cigarette*) Will you?

WIFE: (*Keeping her distance*) No, thanks. (*More boldly*) I never touch it.

Chuckling, HE *produces a lighter, lights up, and settles back comfortably, blowing a cloud of smoke ceilingwards to her astonishment.*

CALLER: Sometime you must come and visit me. You and your husband, of course. I live just over that mountain there. (*Gesturing over his shoulder*) Rigged up a little pot still in my back lot, a crude effort I must confess, but it produces amazingly good stuff. You try some of that, and you'll find your aqua pura pretty un-interesting. *(He regards her a moment; She is quite bewildered. Looking about the room)* Nice little place you have here.

WIFE: *(Easing a trifle)* Thanks. We…

CALLER: Haven't fixed it up much, have you?

WIFE: *(Confused again and somewhat indignant)* Fixed it up? We've always found it quite satisfactory just the way it…

CALLER: *(Pleasantly)* Oh, no offense! *De gustibus* and all that sort of thing, you know. Personally I wasn't at all content with my place the way I found it. Not enough color, if you know what I mean. *(He waits to see if this registers; it doesn't)* No; I guess you don't. Anyway, you must come and see it. At last, after I don't know how many years, I've got it looking something like home. Worked like the very devil on it, let me tell you. *(Rising and going up to the window; wistfully)* Of course, it isn't home; there's no getting around that.

WIFE: Home?

CALLER: *(With a gesture towards the radio)* Don't you ever get tired of that tune?

WIFE: *(Rather on the defensive)* No; I like it.

CALLER: You can get other stations, you know.

WIFE: *(Taking issue)* We have always been satisfied with…

CALLER: Sure, sure. But the trouble with you is you lack the spirit of adventure. Why don't you turn that knob just for the fun of it and see what happens? Aren't you curious? *(She is, yet She hesitates)* Go on; I dare you.

Goaded by him, She turns the dial. The music cuts out, and after a moment of static, a Voice comes over clearly.

RADIO NEWSCASTER: …troops advanced against stiff opposition in the west and central sectors, penetrating enemy defensive positions and capturing several small villages. In the east, activity was confined to reconnaissance patrols. Official casualty lists have been issued, corrected to the end of the past month and indicating that the total of dead, wounded, and missing has…

CALLER: *(Slumping despondently onto the window seat)* Turn it off! Turn it off!

SHE *does so.*

WIFE: What was that?

CALLER: Earth.

WIFE: Really? I didn't know there were people there too.

CALLER: *(Wondering)* Then you really don't remember?

WIFE: You said that before, and he, on the radio, he's always saying that. Tell me what I am supposed to remember.

CALLER: I'll tell you a little story. Perhaps that will remind you.

WIFE: *(Delightedly)* Good! I like stories. *(A courteous afterthought)* And I'll try very hard to be reminded.

SHE *settles down to listen.* HE *tells his story slowly and pointedly, gazing at her intently and pausing between sentences the better to judge her reaction.* SHE *is thoroughly absorbed, but quite evidently her memory is not stirred in the slightest.*

CALLER: Once upon a time there was a man on Earth, so worked up over its wickedness that he went about in a hair shirt, preaching the planet's inevitable destruction. After a time, he advertised that he had built a space ship and would take in it with him any and all who repented of their wrong-doings and wished to escape the Earth's catastrophe. Under the rule of his benevolence they would live, he promised them, a blessed life of purity and innocence and perfect goodness in the sanctuary of the Moon. On the day appointed for his departure in the space ship, the people came in throngs to the launching ground; but when they saw his rocket and what a ridiculous, precarious contraption it was, of scraps and carpet tacks and baling wire, one by one the applicants all demurred. At the last moment, each and every one thought of something he had forgotten to do, an appointment to keep, a letter to write, a friend to be met at the station. A pot, unattended, would boil over on someone's stove, and in some deserted house a light had been left burning. So they all went their separate ways home, all but one couple only. One man and his wife were so fatigued with the Earth's sorrow they were glad to take their chances on the Moon, and, risking everything, they went with him.

WIFE: (*After a pause, ingenuously*) And did they make it? I've never seen them here.

CALLER: It's wonderful, truly wonderful! How he's got you! Oh, the power of the man! The magnetism! The hypnotism! The mesmerism! The enchantment of him! I tell you, it's amazing!

Alarmed and bewildered by the violence of this outburst, SHE *has edged around below the table and is crossing rapidly toward the door, right.*

CALLER: (*Rather sharply; pulling himself together and rising*) Where are you going?

WIFE: (*At the door; timidly*) I... I thought I should call my husband.

CALLER: (*More gently; referring to his watch*) No; don't disturb him. He'll be talking to the Governor now.

WIFE: How do you know that?

CALLER: Doesn't he always at this time?

WIFE: But...

CALLER: That's all right: I've seen the Governor's schedule. "Cool of the evening: walk in man's garden."

WIFE: (*Eagerly*) You know him then?

CALLER: Who, the Governor? Of course I know him. The Master Chef, Chief Electrician, Pilot, Head Sanitary Engineer, Surgeon General, Grand Muckimuck, Poobah, and High Cockalorum! I know him well; as a matter of fact, I used to work for him.

WIFE: You don't say! My husband does odd jobs for him now and again, you know.

CALLER: Oh, my job was full-time.

WIFE: How very lucky you were!

CALLER: Well, yes and no. The work's all right, and he pays you well; but there's no chance for advancement. You can get as far as Vice-President, and there you sit. Have a few ideas of your own and, first thing you know, you're out on your ear. That's what happened to me.

WIFE: *(Gently reproving)* But his ideas are usually right, aren't they?

CALLER: I suppose, as far as you're concerned, they always are. *(At the window)* Yet, he was wrong in one thing; the Earth's still there. They're still fighting over it, tearing it apart, digging it up, treading it down, and blowing it to bits six ways to breakfast; yet, though it may not last forever, it's right there now. And in the midst of all that blood and agony, still there are corners of kindness and pockets out of the way where men of good will persist in making inconclusive gestures of bravery and love. And still the brooks come out of the hills in spring rejoicing, and in winter, when the sun has just gone down, the shadows on the snow are the color of violets. The Earth's still there. Ninety-nine percent of it is acting like Hell, but one percent is aspiring to Heaven; and for my money, that little one percent makes the whole game worth the candle.

WIFE: And once you were on the Earth?

CALLER: *(Still dreaming at the window)* Ah, yes.

WIFE: *(Breaking the spell)* Then, if you liked it so much, why did you come here, however you came?

CALLER: I came on the same ship that brought you, which you don't remember. I didn't count myself among the passengers, because I was employed by the Governor at the time. I was co-pilot, assistant navigator, second communications officer. And I came here because... well, I really don't know why myself, I suppose I came simply because I was curious to see what it was like to live on the Moon.

WIFE: And you're not satisfied with the life here?

CALLER: That's just the trouble with it: it's altogether too satisfactory. I like the process of achieving satisfaction, but for satisfaction itself I don't give two hoots. "Satisfied", in my language, is just another way of saying "dead". Look at you here: you may live here forever or perhaps you will be dead forever. Whatever you call it, it will be just the same. Everything is the same for you. You say and do the same things every day. In a moment now, your husband will come through that door at precisely the same time that he always comes in, and he will have picked two star-fruit and a bunch of leaves for a salad, which you have had for every dinner you have ever eaten here. When he gives them to you, he will make the same corny crack about Lunar Lettuce and Melons of the Moon he always makes, and you will laugh and chide him gently, saying, "What kept you so long?" And he will tell you he has been talking with the Governor, and you will sit down with him while he repeats the same tidbits of the boss's propaganda you heard yesterday and the day before that and every day before. There never can be any difference, because you are always satisfied and never want more, nor less. In this death-life of blessed satisfaction, everything's much too simple for my taste. I like shades and mixtures and perplexities; I welcome challenges and complications. But you don't seem to mind that everything is set forth for you in black and white. Of course, you're presumed to have the power and right to choose at any time according to your own free will, but you know perfectly well the cards are forever stacked in the Governor's favor. You always pick the right answer, and naturally it's always, always, always the same.

WIFE: But it never seems the same.

CALLER: *(Thoroughly dejected)* That's what I can't figure out! I thought I knew all his works and ways, but he has a power over you that passes my understanding.

HE *reflects on this a moment, unhappily, as* SHE *hovers by, unsure what, if any, gesture of sympathy is expected of her.* HE *resolves her problem with a sudden shake of head and shrug of his shoulders. Rousing himself,* HE *again refers to his watch. It's getting late.*

Here now! I've overstayed my moment. I must be getting along.

WIFE: What a pity! Won't you stay until my husband comes back; I know he'd be very disappointed to miss you.

CALLER: I'll be seeing him soon enough. You're both coming to visit me, aren't you? The first place you see over the mountain. In fact, the only one.

WIFE: You're very kind. *(Getting an idea)* But look you have so far to go, and it's late already; why not stay and have dinner with us?

CALLER: Now you are very kind, but I tell you, madam, in all candor, I should rather fry eternally in Hell than face another star-fruit.

WIFE: *(Disappointed)* Oh.

CALLER: But I thank you, and I thank you especially for reminding me of something I had quite forgotten. *(Fishing in his pocket)* I've brought you a present.

WIFE: How very nice!

CALLER: Perhaps just this once you might like to try a little variety in your diet.

HE *produces an apple, which* HE *offers to her with a flourish.*

WIFE: What in Heaven's name is that?

CALLER: Better to ask, "What on Earth is that?"; for this, like you and me, is a child of Earth. I had one in my pocket on the space ship. Put it there to nibble on on the way, but I guess I was so taken up with the scenery and all that I never got around to eating it. One day, a long time after, when the Moon had begun to pall and I had seen all the scenery I wanted to see a thousand times over, I was rummaging among my things, and I came upon the ancestor of this apple, all brown and withered out of recognition. I took the seeds and planted them in my garden. That was the day I began my lunar labors and life again was interesting. This fruit is the symbol of my hard work and my happiness. I want you to have it to eat in remembrance of me.

HE *puts it on the plate on the table.*

WIFE: *(Hesitating)* Thank you. Thank you very much, but…

CALLER: Yes?

WIFE: I don't think I can have this. The Surgeon General has warned us against eating any unusual food unless he particularly recommends it. I really shouldn't…

CALLER: Nonsense! Anyone can tell you, "An apple a day keeps the doctor away." And even if it doesn't have all the vitamins of star-fruit, it tastes a damn sight better. *(Covering HER attempted protest)* Well, now I really must be going. I kiss your hand. *(HE does so, startling her somewhat)* Good-bye.

HE *crosses to the door;* SHE *looks after him, rubbing the hand* HE *has kissed.*

WIFE: *(Scarcely audible)* Good-bye.

CALLER: *(Turning at the door)* And one more thing I forgot to mention: you know what the Governor is always saying about being able to return if ever you so desire? Well, that's his little plug for me. I've taken over the rocket, you know. Fixed it up in grand shape. If you ever decide you want to go back to Earth, come to me; I'll be running the return trip. I'll be seeing you!

HE *goes out.* SHE *has put up her hand to wave farewell, but the door closes behind him before* SHE *can complete the gesture.*

When HE *has gone, exhausted by his bewildering volubility,* SHE *sinks with a sigh into the chair, right of the table. Slowly her head turns, and* SHE *is staring at the apple, astonishingly red against the white plate and white table cloth. Idly intrigued,* SHE *reaches her hand out toward it, touches it, picks it up; then, suddenly horrified,* SHE *returns it to the plate and withdraws her hand.* SHE *rises and crosses to the sideboard, as if making a conscious effort to avoid looking at the table's strange burden.* SHE *turns on the radio; there is a momentary cacophony of incomprehensible noises which* SHE *swiftly rectifies by turning the station-selector. The Moon music comes up, simple and clear.* SHE *is again relaxed; but not for long: the attraction of the table is all compelling, and as* SHE *turns again to look, the stitch apparently returns to her left side, and her hand goes up to it.* SHE *does not seem to notice now that the music over the radio is becoming, by degrees, more and more sour and out-of-key, as though it were on a record running down; it is punctuated by increasingly violent bursts of static. Impulsively,* SHE *reaches out and, taking up a knife, cuts the apple in two. Leaving one half on the plate,* SHE *carries the other to her mouth and bites into it furiously. The shock of one just coming out of blindness, a mixture of delight and terror at being confronted with an utterly unfamiliar situation.* SHE *gazes about the room as though* SHE *had never seen it before; the remnant of her half of the apple falls to the floor. Finally, the insistent distress of the radio commands her attention.* SHE *turns the dial, and at length the newscaster's voice comes over clear.*

RADIO NEWSCASTER: …Red Cross and government agencies have sped rescue teams to the stricken area. Unconfirmed reports place the death toll at 57 with over 100 persons missing and countless numbers homeless. Flood waters are not expected to reach their crest until…

SHE *tries another station and tunes in a swing band; the music is brash, jazzy, and monotonous.* SHE *is fascinated for a moment, then tries another.* SHE *is startled by a loud explosion of laughter, applause, and cheers; the voice of a quizmaster, in the frenzy of triumph, strains above the enthusiasm of the crowd.*

RADIO QUIZMASTER: She's done it, ladies and gentlemen! She's done it! Mrs. Caroline Kopplemans, the eighty-seven-year-old great grandmother from Rahway, New Jersey, HAS JUST SHOT THE MOON!

This alarming information urges her to turn the dial again. SHE *is rewarded by assorted squawks, signals, and fragments of voices, until, with unexpected clarity and almost unbearably loud, the strains of the finale of Beethoven's Seventh Symphony sweep in upon her. Frantically* SHE *tries to turn down the volume, but succeeds only increasing it. The fury of the music swirls about her, exhausting her. At last the radio itself seems taxed beyond its powers and protests with irate poppings and cracklings.* SHE *is finally able to turn it off; and, her hands propped on the sideboard,* SHE *leans over the silent radio, breathing heavily, her body racked with sobs.*

There is a knock at the door. SHE *turns as though to answer it and notices the remaining half apple on its plate, which* SHE *makes haste to conceal in the cupboard, left. The knocking persists.* SHE *staggers over to the door, opens it, and stands by abjectly, lowering her tear-stained face. Her* HUSBAND *enters cheerfully, passing her. In his arms are two large star-fruit, the size and shape of honeydew melons, white with black stars upon them; in one hand* HE *carries several large, white leaves.*

MAN: Here, madam, is your Lunar Lettuce.

HE *drops the leaves onto the table, then turns forward, holding a star-fruit in each hand, admiringly.*

MAN: And here: your Cosmic Cantaloupes, your Astral Avocados, your Planetary Pomegranates, your Melons of the Moon!

Somewhat contemptuously, as HE *puts them on the table.*

Your star-fruit.

SHE *has closed the door and is leaning against it, her forehead propped upon her arm. When* HE *makes his now too-familiar jest,* SHE *turns toward him, her face registering exasperation, and turns away again.*

WIFE: *(Speaking into the door)* You were talking with the Governor.

MAN: *(Surprised)* How did you know that?

WIFE: You do every evening,

MAN: *(Puzzled)* Huh…? Yes, he was saying…

WIFE: I know what he said.

MAN: *(Not sure he has heard her correctly)* What's that?

SHE *faces him; shocked at her appearance,* HE *moves toward her.*

Honey, what has happened?

SHE *runs to him and throws her arms about him with an unaccustomed fury that bewilders him.*

WIFE: *(Sobbing again)* Hold me! Hold me!

MAN: I'll... I'll get the Surgeon General.

WIFE: *(Breaking from him)* No; don't. There's nothing he can do now.

Crossing him; pausing at the table.

While you were talking to the Governor, I had a visitor too.

MAN: Who?

WIFE: He didn't say. He seemed to think I should have remembered him.

MAN: That's ridiculous: there's never been anyone here but us and the Governor. Why didn't you ask his name?

WIFE: *(With some irritation)* I couldn't very well. *(More gently)* He talked so much and confused me so, I never thought of asking.

MAN: *(Ribbing her, not unpleasantly)* Fine secretary you'd make!

WIFE: *(Ignoring this; absorbed in her own thoughts)* He was right, you know. I can't recall his name, but I'm sure now I have seen him somewhere before.

Before HE *can speak,* SHE *goes to the cupboard and takes out the plate with the remaining half apple.*

WIFE: He brought us a present. Something to eat. Something for a change.

Putting it on the table before him.

MAN: What in Heaven's that?

WIFE: I asked that too, but there is no name for it in Heaven. It's an apple. That's your share, if you want it. I've eaten mine.

MAN: You shouldn't have, you know. The Surgeon General has specifically warned us against ...

WIFE: I know. But I've eaten it just the same. I was... I guess I was curious.

MAN: *(In a tone of superiority)* And you've gone and made yourself ill for the first time in your life. I'd better call the doctor.

HE *starts to go.*

WIFE: I tell you there's nothing he can do. I know that very well. Here.

HER *hand to her heart.*

I'm not ill. It's just that I can remember things now.

MAN: *(Having stopped)* What things?

WIFE: Where we were before we came here.

MAN: We never were anywhere before we...

WIFE: Oh, yes, we were. We were there.

Pointing to the sky and the crescent Earth above the mountains.

On the Earth.

MAN: You're not just sick; you're crazy!

WIFE: *(With mirthless laughter)* I thought the man in the tweed suit was crazy too, until I tasted that.

The apple.

And when I did, how the memories came flooding in upon me, filling me till I thought that I should burst! I remembered colors then.

A pause.

No; of course you don't understand; no more did I. But look here.

Pointing to the apple again.

What color is that? See! You don't know any more than I knew once. Red is a riddle for you, but eat the apple and you will learn the answer. And you will remember, too, other things that must now be only mysteries and make you think I'm talking madness: how trees are green, skies blue, corn yellow. Those are simple colors for beginners. Then you will know all the shades that glimmer in the rainbow and the vast, vast, ever-changing color and no-color of the sea. But now you can't even imagine a sea. So very unlike the fountain here in our Moon garden! All that watery waste, so terrible, so beautiful, and so undrinkable! Eat that, and you understand.

HIS *hand goes tentatively toward the apple, but suddenly, frantically,* SHE *grabs his wrist, preventing him.*

WIFE: No! No; don't! I can remember more. How complicated our life was there! We had no Governor, no Master Chef or Surgeon General to tell us what to do. And choice was never a simple matter of this or that, black and white – one always altogether right, the other clearly wrong. On Earth there were too many choices, and every one had something good in it and much that was bad. We tried, when we had to make up our minds, to pick whatever at the time seemed best; but no sooner had we chosen than we recalled the good in other possibilities, which we had put aside forever. Then we yearned for what we could not have and knew a kind of desire that grows nowhere on the Moon. Here "I want" is a command, satisfied almost in its uttering; there, "I want" is a lifelong cry of unrelieved and unrelievable despair.

MAN: *(Withdrawing his hand)* I should not like to learn that cry.

WIFE: Don't eat the apple then.

MAN: No; I must not, I will not.

WIFE: *(Behind him; gently)* You are very wise and right. Stay here always.

MAN: *(Rather pompously, as though her remark were obvious)* Of course: it's better that we should.

WIFE: It's better that *you* should; but I must go.

MAN: *(Confused)* Go? Where?

Where SHE *is standing* HE *cannot see her tears.*

WIFE: To the man in the tweed suit, my visitor. He's taken over the space ship... but, no; you don't remember the space ship.

MAN: *(With irritation)* I certainly don't, and I don't know what you're talking about. What have you to do with this man?

WIFE: *(Painfully)* Darling, how can I find an easy way to tell you? He's taking me back to Earth. I'm leaving you.

MAN: *(Shocked)* Leaving!

Plaintively.

But what have I done?

WIFE: You have done nothing.

MAN: *(Anger mounting)* Your fellow in the tweed suit, then: he's been up to something. Where is he now? Wait till I...

WIFE: *(Somewhat exasperated)* Don't be silly. Anything that has been done, I have done myself.

MAN: *(Exploding)* "Silly?" Just because of that ridiculous, what-do-you-call-it, fruit, you talk about leaving me forever. Who's silly now?

WIFE: *(Wretchedly)* I wish I could explain it to you, but you'd never understand. Believe me I would stay, if it were possible at all. But now, turn away; it will be easier for me to go.

SHE turns him around so that HE *is facing the table;* SHE *puts her lips gently to his shoulder, then breaks from him, taking a step backward toward the door.*

WIFE: You will forget me, as you have forgotten everything.

If HE *seems indifferent to her parting, it is because* HE *is concentrating on the apple before him.* SHE *has reached the door, when* HE *seizes the fruit and, turning, stops her, calling out.*

MAN: Wait! Wait! Look what I'm doing! I'm eating your dammed, fool apple...

HE *has taken a bite out of it, triumphantly, as if to prove her unreasonableness, but having tasted it,* HE *sinks into the chair with a sigh, defeated and understanding.* SHE *is smiling, sympathetic and immensely pleased.*

WIFE: Now you know.

MAN: I know.

WIFE: *(Prompting)* And you remember...?

MAN: *(Miserably)* I remember an eternity of boredom.

WIFE: We called it, once, tranquility.

MAN: Peace.

WIFE: Heaven.

MAN: How could we have?

WIFE: Ah, that is the mystery.

MAN: *(Wretchedly)* Yes.

Pause.

Things will be more difficult here from now on.

WIFE: Difficult? Impossible.

MAN: Not necessarily, do you think? It will take some getting used to our new situation, but we must learn to manage.

HE *gives serious thought to the problem.* SHE *regards him incredulously.*

WIFE: Are you serious?

MAN: Hmh?

WIFE: Do you believe for a moment that we can stay here after this? I saw from the start it was out of the question. Not that it will be easy to go, though better now that I shan't have to go alone.

MAN: *(Patronizingly)* Oh, you're so impulsive; and you forget your own lessons. What of that "cry of despair"? Do you want to go back to that?

WIFE: I said it wouldn't be easy, but look at the alternative: On Earth, at least, there were distractions, small changes in themselves but enough to make life bearable. Flowers surprised us and flights of birds. Old friends called unexpectedly and brought with them new acquaintances. In the midst of our larger desperation, we lived on little hopes. Something inside us said, "Tomorrow, if things aren't any better, at any rate they may be different." We were often bored, but there was always the chance that we wouldn't be. Here there is no chance, no hope; we know that tomorrow will be exactly like today and yesterday.

MAN: *(Petulantly)* That sameness didn't bother us in the past.

WIFE: When we remembered no experience of change.

MAN: *(His conviction failing)* Perhaps the Governor will fix it so that we'll forget again.

WIFE: *(Relentless)* We gave him our word once to follow him; now we've broken it. Should we expect him to take us on again?

MAN: He'll forgive us. I'm sure... I think he would.

WIFE: He would. Than all that talk of our free will is meaningless, if our choice need have no consequences.

MAN: *(Rashly)* What do I care about my will? I'd give it up in a minute. If only he'd...

WIFE: *(After a pause; scornfully)* Haven't you any pride?

SHE *glares at him, and* HE *looks away, sheepishly.* SHE *crosses to the door with exaggerated purposefulness.*

WIFE: *(Elaborately casual)* Well, perhaps it won't be very hard for me to go alone after all.

MAN: *(Agitatedly)* No! No! Don't talk like that; I...

SHE *stops.*

Wait a moment.

WIFE: *(Quietly; with a smile)* I'm right, aren't I? You knew it all the time.

MAN: *(Thoroughly ashamed of himself)* You're right.

To himself; angrily.

Oh, God! Oh, God!

WIFE: Cheer up: it isn't as bad as all that. We had some good times back there at home; perhaps we shall have some again.

As SHE speaks SHE crosses to the radio. SHE turns it on, and it obliges with an Offenbach waltz, soft and sentimental. SHE then goes behind her husband where HE is sitting and puts her hands upon his shoulders, consoling.

WIFE: Do you remember when we were young? I lived in the white house with the elm tree in the front yard.

HE *is sulking;* SHE *coaxes him.*

Oh, come on! Play the game, if only for my sake.

MAN: *(Somewhat grudgingly)* I lived in the red one next door, where the honeysuckle grew over the verandah.

WIFE: Behind our house was my father's orchard. How proud he was of his apples! They won first prize at the state fair three years running.

MAN: *(Beginning to get into the spirit of the game)* He was always fussing about them.

WIFE: And we were always trying to pick them before they were ready.

MAN: *(Imitating)* "You kids keep clear of them apples till they're ripe, unless you're fig'ring on spending your holidays in bed with the colic."

SHE *laughs.*

WIFE: That boy from across the street, the one with the red hair, he tried to tell us they were better green. He dared me to taste one, and I did.

MAN: What a regular little devil he was!

WIFE: *(More to herself: with sudden recognition)* Wasn't he, though!

MAN: When your father found you out, he gave you a licking.

WIFE: And you comforted me.

MAN: *(With a twinkle in his eye)* In the hayloft over the barn.

WIFE: Yes, indeed! That was the first time I learned about...

With mock indignation.

What a naughty boy! What a naughty boy!

Bending over him to snuggle her cheek against his ear, SHE stretches her arms down over his chest, hugging him to her. HIS hands travel up along her arms, relishing her attentions. THEY begin to laugh, at first with some embarrass-

ment. SHE *encourages him by tickling.* THEY *laugh in uproarious unison until they are exhausted; then* HE *breaks from her grasp and rises.*

MAN: *(Wiping the tears from his eyes, sobering)* Well, shall we start?

WIFE: *(Brightly)* Back to Earth!

MAN: *(Suddenly serious)* To Earth. To toil and pain, to fear and hatred, and to death.

WIFE: *(Softly)* And on winter evenings: snow the color of violets.

MAN: *(Not having heard her)* How's that?

WIFE: Would you rather stay here?

MAN: No. Not now.

WIFE: *(Gently)* We'll make the best of it somehow.

HE *acknowledges this with a wry smile and turns to open the door. Looking out,* HE *stops short.*

MAN: Uhoh! The Governor.

WIFE: *(Looking out past his shoulder)* With a scowl on his face like thunder.

MAN: He knows.

WIFE: *(Not well concealing her apprehension)* If he doesn't, we'll have to tell him.

MAN: *(Mischievously, but also fearing)* Would you like to? You always had a special way with him.

WIFE: Not on your life!

MAN: *(Squaring himself for the ordeal)* Come then; we'll go together.

THEY *walk out, arm in arm. The radio, left playing in the deserted house, has dimmed almost to imperceptibility. The sound, as it comes up again, is the same simple and somewhat soporific music of the Moon that introduced the play.*

CURTAIN

CONTRADANCE

a romantic play

Contradance

A performance of *Contradance* was presented at Polaris North in 1993, as part of an evening of one-acts by various playwrights. Leslie Lynn Meeker directed a cast consisting of Chris Burmeister and Rebecca Vernooy.

cast

HE

SHE

set

Two rooms, each the mirror image of the other; a door in the wall between them. The furniture of either room is the same; the decor, quite different.

The bed in His room is a simple iron cot with thin mattress and spring. It is unmade: the sheets are soiled and rumpled; the dented pillow is askew; the threadbare blanket, sliding to the floor. HER bed is covered with a pink, tufted spread, neatly arranged; the pillow is plumped; a couple of small, frilly souvenir pillows and a teddy bear with a pink ribbon around his neck are carefully arranged at the head of the bed.

HIS table and the kitchen chair drawn up to it are bare, unpainted, and scarred with cigarette burns. HER table is covered in sateen, skirted as a dressing table; HER chair has been freshly and gaily painted.

Over HIS table hangs a naked light bulb at the end of a fraying wire. A similar light over HER table is fitted with a pink, fringed shade.

HIS easy chair is soiled and dilapidated; the upholstery is worn, and some of the stuffing is exposed. HER easy chair may be in no better condition essentially, but it is covered with a bright, clean, flowered slip-cover.

In each room, the accessories carry out this pattern of contrast.

In the far corner of each room is a large, irregularly shaped object covered by a sheet. HIS sheet is gray and wrinkled, but carefully draped. HERS is white and freshly ironed, but rather casually flung over the concealed object.

The lights are on in both rooms. HE *is pacing about his room.* HE *sits down, gets up, lies down on the bed, gets up. Meanwhile* SHE, *in her room, is trying to look through the keyhole of the door between them.* SHE *turns off her light and returns to the keyhole.* HE *is standing, supporting himself by the back of the kitchen chair, staring vacantly down at the table. The door, under her inadvertent pressure, opens – swinging into his room.* HE *looks up, startled.*

HE: Yes?

SHE: *(Embarrassed; peering through the partially opened door)* I'm sorry. I pushed against it, I guess. It just opened.

HE: Oh.

SHE: I'll close it again.

SHE *begins to close it slowly.*

HE: *(Before the door is fully shut)* Wait a minute!

SHE: *(Flinging the door wide open)* Yes?

HE: *(Looking at* HER*)* Oh. *(Shyly)* Hello.

SHE: Hello. *(Pause)* I live next door.

HE: Do you? *(Pause)* I live here.

SHE: I know.

HE: It isn't much of a place, but...

SHE: *(Eagerly)* Yes?

HE: I was going to say: Come in if you want to.

SHE: *(Stepping into* HIS *room)* Thank you; I might, but just for a moment.

HE: It isn't much of a place.

SHE: *(After closing the door behind* HER*)* I think it's very nice.

HE: No, it isn't. You're just being polite.

SHE: Not at all. I think you have everything very nicely arranged.

HE: Do you really?

SHE: Oh, yes; very nicely.

HE: I live by myself, you see.

SHE: I see.

HE: I haven't felt it was necessary to make the place very fancy. Just for me, you see.

SHE: Simplicity is the first principle of good interior design.

HE: You think so?

SHE: Oh, yes. Simplicity. The first principle.

SHE *has wandered over to the bed and, unobtrusively, is drawing the pillow into position.*

HE: That's my bed.

SHE: *(Startled; letting go of the pillow)* Oh, really?

HE: And this is my chair. And my table.

HE stands behind the kitchen chair and stares moodily at the table. HIS back is to HER. SHE takes the opportunity, hastily and surreptitiously, to arrange the pillow and draw up the blanket. HE looks up at the light.

That's my light. The cord is frayed.

SHE: *(Coming up behind HIM)* I see.

HE: *(Turning away abruptly)* This is another chair. More comfortable than that one.

Unobserved, SHE sweeps HER hand across the table, blows the dust off HER hand. SHE comes down beside HIM.

SHE: It's a nice chair.

HE: Won't you sit down? It's more comfortable.

SHE: Thank you.

SHE sits.

HE: Will you have a cigarette?

SHE: Thank you.

There is a packet of cigarettes on the table. HE turns to get it. SHE rises suddenly.

Excuse me. I must get something.

SHE goes to the door.

I'll only be a minute.

HE: Come back.

SHE: I'll be right back.

SHE goes into HER room and closes the door. SHE turns on HER light. Frantically, SHE searches for something on the table. Not there. On the bed. Not there. Under the bed. SHE takes out a suitcase. SHE takes a purse out of the suitcase and a cigarette holder out of the purse. SHE puts the cigarette holder aside and takes a compact out of the purse. Hastily, SHE powders HER nose, primps HER hair in the compact mirror. SHE returns the compact to the purse; the purse, to the suitcase; the suitcase, to under the bed. SHE takes up the cigarette holder, turns off the light, smoothes HER dress, goes to the door. Meanwhile, HE looks nervously about HIS room. HE goes to the bed and makes it, tucking in and smoothing the blanket. HE blows the dust off the table. HE plumps the cushion of the easy chair. HE is finished before SHE is. HE stands in the middle of the room, surveying HIS work. Waiting, HE becomes dejected. SHE raps softly at the door.

HE: *(Brightening)* Come in.

SHE: *(Entering; closing the door behind HER)* Hello again.

HE: I was afraid you wouldn't be back.

SHE: I said I'd come back.

HE: I know; but I was afraid you wouldn't.

SHE: You mustn't be afraid.

SHE *sits in the easy chair, crossing* HER *knees.* *Pause.*

HE: You're beautiful.

SHE: Thank you.

SHE *draws the edge of* HER *skirt down over* HER *knees, carefully.*

HE: I fixed up the room while you were gone.

SHE: Did you?

HE: Well, a little.

SHE: It's very nice.

HE: Thank you.

Pause.

SHE: You offered me a cigarette.

HE: Oh, yes, of course. I'm sorry.

HE *gets the pack from the table, offers it to* HER. SHE *takes a cigarette, places it in* HER *holder, puts the holder in* HER *mouth.* HE *lights a match for* HER. HIS *hand is shaking;* SHE *steadies it as* SHE *lights* HER *cigarette. As the cigarette is being lit:*

You're beautiful.

SHE: Thank you. Have you an ashtray?

HE: Just use the floor.

SHE: Oh, I shouldn't think of doing that.

HE *is momentarily dismayed; then* HE *gets a saucer from the table.*

This is all I have.

SHE: It's very nice.

SHE *is looking neither at* HIM *nor at the saucer.* SHE *is looking at the shrouded object across the room, as* SHE *smokes nonchalantly.*

HE: What are you looking at?

SHE: *(Still looking)* Nothing.

HE: It's just something I keep covered up.

SHE: Why do you keep it covered?

HE: Let's not talk about that.

HE *brings the kitchen chair over and sits on it.*

SHE: You shouldn't keep anything covered.

HE: Let's talk about you.

SHE: *(Stroking* HIS *cheek)* You mustn't be afraid.

HE: Your hand is soft.

SHE *withdraws* HER *hand.*

I'm sorry.

SHE: What are you sorry about?

HE: Your hand.

SHE: There's no need to be sorry.

SHE *puts a hand on* HIS *knee.*

HE: *(Grinning)* Gee!

But SHE *is staring at the covered object.* HE *rises abruptly.*

Would you like a drink?

HE *returns* HIS *chair to its original position at the table.*

SHE: No, thank you. I'd better not.

HE: *(Taking a bottle of wine from the table)* Why not?

SHE: *(Looking at the covered object)* I don't drink.

HE: It's only a domestic wine.

SHE: *(Going to* HIM*)* You don't have to entertain me.

SHE *takes the bottle from* HIM *and returns it to the table.* HE *attempts to embrace* HER. SHE *breaks away, sits on the edge of the bed.*

Let's play a game.

HE: I'm afraid I don't know any games.

SHE: Afraid again?

HE: Well...

SHE: I make you nervous.

HE: No; I feel completely at ease.

HE *sits in the easy chair.*

SHE: Associations.

HE: What?

SHE: A game. Associations. I say a word, and then you say a word.

HE: *(Making a joke)* Say the word!

SHE *laughs; then, suddenly:*

SHE: Love.

HE: *(Quickly)* You.

SHE: *(Quickly)* Bed.

HE: *(Quickly)* You.

SHE: *(Quickly)* Table.

HE: *(Quickly)* Chair.

SHE: *(After a pause)* Varnish.

HE: Huh?

SHE: V-a-r-n-i-s-h: varnish.

HE: *(Quickly)* Egg.

SHE: *(After a pause)* Love.

HE: *(Quickly)* Woman.

SHE: *(Quickly)* Bed.

HE: *(Quickly)* Woman.

SHE: *(Quickly)* Avalanche.

HE: *(Quickly)* Aluminum hydroxide.

SHE: *(Quickly)* Woman.

HE: *(After a pause)* Beauty.

SHE: *(Quickly)* Love.

HE: *(Quickly)* Beauty.

SHE: *(Very deliberately; after a pause)* Bed.

HE: *(Quickly)* Sleep.

SHE: *(Quickly; rising)* Let's dance.

HE: *(Rising)* There's no music.

> SHE *goes to* HIM, *singing a waltz tune, and sweeps* HIM *into a dance.*

SHE: La, la, la-la, etc.

> *As* THEY *twirl past the covered object,* SHE *turns* HER *head to look at it and, missing a step, trips* HIM.

HE: *(Recovering; continuing to dance)* I don't dance very well.

SHE: You dance divinely.

HE: No; not really.

SHE: *(Unsuccessfully grabbing at the covered object as* SHE *twirls past)* Fred Astaire.

HE: *(Stepping on* HER *foot)* Thank you.

SHE: *(Breaking from* HIM; *stopping the dance)* I'll have that drink now.

HE: *(At the table)* It's only a domestic wine.

SHE: The wines of New York are well regarded by connoisseurs.

> *On the table are a tumbler and a coffee cup.* HE *is about to pour into the glass, notices it is dirty, surreptitiously cleans it out with* HIS *finger.*

HE: This wine is from California.

SHE: Connoisseurs well regard the wines of California.

HE: *(Pouring and handing* HER *the glass)* Thank you.

SHE: You poured so much. I'll be tipsy.

HE: *(Pouring for* HIMSELF, *into the cup)* You don't have to drink it all if you don't want to.

SHE: *(Holding up* HER *glass)* What a beautiful color! "The Grape that can with logic absolute/ The Two-and-Seventy jarring Sects confute: / The sovereign Alchemist that in a trice/ Life's leaden metal into Gold transmute!"

HE: *(Delighted)* The Rubaiyat!

SHE: *(Twirling from* HIM) But I don't know what it means.

HE: Well, you see, the seventy-two jarring sects were...

SHE: *(Hastily, raising* HER *glass)* To us!

HE: *(Raising* HIS *cup)* To you!

HE *sips from* HIS *cup.* SHE *drains* HER *glass in one draught, then flings the glass in the air. It falls, shattering.* SHE *stands, facing* HIM *across the room, in an attitude of triumph.* HE *is stunned, staring first at* HER, *then past* HER *at the covered object.* HIS *hand, holding the cup, begins to tremble.* HE *sets the cup down.*

Look at it.

SHE: No; I'd better not.

HE: Go ahead: look at it.

SHE: Everyone must have his secret.

HE: There must be no secrets between us. Our lives must be completely open to each other. I must be entirely at your mercy.

SHE: And I, at yours.

HE: Then look.

SHE: All right, then.

SHE *moves toward it.* HE *begins to panic.*

HE: Of course...

SHE: Yes?

HE: If you really think...

SHE: Oh, but I think...I mean...

HE: *(Defeated)* Whatever you think best.

SHE: If I didn't, it would always be between us.

HE: Look. *(Very softly)* Please look.

SHE *smiles, then turns slowly, but deliberately, towards the covered object.* SHE *pauses, then carefully withdraws the sheet.* HE *is trembling. Under the sheet is her image seated on a throne. The flesh, the clothes, the hair – all are dead white. On its head is a golden crown; in its hand is a blood red rose. The eyes are closed.* SHE *gasps.* HER *hand goes to* HER *mouth as though to muffle the sound.* SHE *reaches out and takes the rose from the hand of the image. Touching the flower,* HER *hand comes away red.* SHE *gives a little shriek and drops the rose.* HE *turns away and, supporting* HIMSELF *by the back of the kitchen chair, is shaking with sobs.* SHE *backs away very slowly, staring at the image.*

SHE: *(As* SHE *moves)* It's very beautiful. It's very beautiful. It's very beautiful.

SHE *has reached the door and now notices* HIM, *still sobbing.* SHE *goes to* HIM *and very gently touches* HIS *shoulder.* HE *leaves the chair and clings to* HER, HIS *head upon* HER *breast. Very softly, as* SHE *strokes* HIM:

There, there: I understand.

HE: *(Muffled against* HER*)* Can you forgive me?

SHE: Of course, I always forgive.

SHE *lifts up* HIS *face and looks into* HIS *eyes.*

I always understand.

HE *is no longer crying.* HE *smiles.* HE *moves as though to kiss* HER. SHE *moves away.*

Not now.

Taking HIM *by the hand.*

Come.

Reaching behind HER; *opening the door.*

Come.

Dazed, HE *passes* HER, *goes to the door. In the doorway* HE *stops and would turn around.*

Don't look back.

Obedient, HE *goes into the darkness of* HER *room.* SHE, *however, turns and has a long look at* HIS *room. With* HER *hand,* SHE *tests the table top for dust. It is still dusty.* SHE *smiles, then turns out* HIS *light.*

HE: It's dark. I can't see.

SHE: I'm right here.

In the darkness, SHE *passes into* HER *room, closing the door behind* HER.

HE: *(In panic)* I can't see!

SHE: I'll turn on the light.

SHE *does so.* HE *looks about, smiling – as though* HE *had just awaked in Paradise.*

This is my room.

HE: *(Delighted)* Yes!

SHE *moves about the room as* SHE *names the various objects in it.* HE, *standing in the center of the room, turns in place, noticing no particular object, but enraptured by all.*

SHE: This is my table.

HE: Yes!

SHE: This is my chair.

HE: Yes!

SHE: That is my bed and this is my lamp.

HE: Yes, yes!

SHE: And this is another, more comfortable chair.

HE: It's very beautiful.

SHE stands beside HIM, holding HIS hand. HE continues to look about, musing to HIMSELF: "Very beautiful." Then HE notices the covered object in the corner. Innocently:

What's under there?

SHE: *(Truthfully)* I don't know. I never looked.

HE: *(Dismissing the matter)* I see.

Suddenly HE puts HIS hand to HIS brow, reeling.

SHE: *(Concerned)* What's the matter?

HE: Nothing.

SHE: You're not well.

HE: No; I'm fine.

SHE: You don't look well.

HE: *(Trying to show conviction)* I'm in perfect physical condition.

SHE: You don't know how to take care of yourself. That's what's the trouble.

HE: *(Somewhat petulantly; striding towards the door)* Of course, I know how...

SHE: *(Quickly)* When did you eat last?

This stops HIM.

HE: An hour ago...or two.

Pause. HIS self-assurance is gone.

Maybe three.

SHE: *(Rather smugly)* You see.

HE: I see.

SHE goes to HIM, puts HER hand on HIS brow.

What are you doing?

SHE: Feeling your forehead.

HE: How is it?

SHE: Cold.

With the back of HER hand, SHE feels HIS cheek.

HE: My cheek?

SHE: Hot.

SHE puts HER hand over HIS heart.

HE: My heart?

SHE: *(Matter-of-factly)* Beating.

HE: *(Plaintively)* Help me.

SHE: Come. You'd better lie down.

SHE *leads* HIM, *staggering, over to the bed.*

HE: *(Slumping on the edge of the bed)* I'm sorry.

SHE: There's nothing to be sorry about. Here, put your feet up.

SHE *lifts* HIS *feet onto the bed.* HE *is drowsy, but still sitting up.*

HE: I'm such a trouble to you.

SHE: That's what I'm here for.

HE: *(His head in His hands)* My head.

SHE: *(Removing the teddy bear from the pillow)* There. There. You must rest.

HE: *(Submitting as SHE gently forces HIM to lie back)* Yes. Rest.

SHE *hands* HIM *the teddy bear, which* HE *clutches to* HIM. HIS *eyes are closed.* SHE *sits beside* HIM, *stroking* HIS *hair.*

SHE: Sleep. Sleep.

HE: *(As though in sleep)* Forgive me.

SHE: Of course.

SHE *continues to stroke; and* HE, *to sleep. At last* SHE *stops, but remains sitting awhile beside* HIM. *Then* SHE *looks up, rises, crosses to the door.* SHE *has almost reached the door when* HE *wakes up.*

HE: *(Frantic)* Where are you?

SHE: I'm right here.

HE: Don't leave me!

SHE: I'll be right back.

HE: Don't leave me!

SHE: Sleep. Sleep. Sleep. Sleep. Sleep.

As SHE *speaks, ever more softly,* SHE *slowly opens the door.* SHE *pauses a moment to ascertain that* HE *is sleeping peacefully again, clutching the bear.* SHE *follows the path of light from* HER *room into* HIS. *Swiftly, but quietly,* SHE *crosses to where the rose has fallen.* SHE *picks up the rose and returns to* HER *room, closing the door softly after* HER. SHE *crosses to the bed, extricates the teddy bear from* HIS *grasp and replaces it with the rose, which* HE *clutches as firmly as* HE *did the bear.* HE *does not wake up.*

HE: *(Asleep)* I love you.

SHE: I forgive you.

SHE *picks up the teddy bear and lies down on the bed beside* HIM. *As* SHE *turns toward* HIM – *not touching* HIM, *however* – SHE *tosses the teddy bear aside. The bear, falling, strikes the covered object, dislodging the sheet.* HIS *image is revealed. It is bound by a pink ribbon to a dainty little chair, cushioned with chintz and trimmed with flounces. The greenish face is distorted; the eyeballs bulge; the clothing is torn; the mangled body is splattered with blood.*

CURTAIN

THE EDGE OF THE ABYSS

a one act play

The Edge of the Abyss

A staged performance of this play was given in 1992 at Polaris North. It was directed by Leslie Lynn Meeker with the cast of Chris Burmeister and Tom Williams.

cast

Joey

Buck

set

The scene is described by Joey early in the play, but there is no need for the designer to reproduce this naturalistically. This is a suggestion: Upper right corner of the stage, against the back wall: a table or platform. On top of the table, a step-ladder, the steps descending left. An entrance (plank) leading offstage right from the top of the ladder. The audience should be able to see only the lower part of the legs of anyone standing on the top of the ladder or on the entrance ramp. At the foot of the ladder steps: a long table or platform running from back stage wall almost to footlights. A second table or platform parallel to this – the two platforms being five or six feet apart. Scattered on these platforms: boxes to represent rocks. Connecting these two platforms about four feet from their downstage ends: a plank (the bridge). Downstage of the "bridge", its top adjacent to the second platform, its steps descending right: a small kitchen ladder. Left of the second platform: a space, stage-level. In the background (left): coat racks or other objects to represent trees. Descending from second platform to this area, stage left: a plank or ramp. Exit off left.

JOEY'S VOICE: *(Off right)* Watch it!

BUCK'S VOICE: *(Off right)* What do you mean: watch it?

JOEY'S VOICE: What do you think I mean: watch it? You're going over the edge.

BUCK'S VOICE: By God, you're right! Hey, close!

JOEY'S VOICE: You can say that again.

Pause

Now, where're you going?

BUCK'S VOICE: What do you mean: where am I going?

JOEY'S VOICE: Another step and you run smack into the cliff.

BUCK'S VOICE: Oh.

JOEY'S VOICE: A smidgen to your right now.

Pause

No, goddamit: can't you tell right from left yet? ...That's it... Not too much or over we go.... There. Take it easy now... Step... Step... Now you've got it.

BUCK'S *feet appear at the top of the ladder, and a pole that he is carrying.*

BUCK: I'm going to stop here.

JOEY'S VOICE: *(Above)* You'd better a moment: the going gets rough here.

BUCK: What happens?

JOEY'S VOICE: Well, first we go down.

BUCK: Steep?

JOEY'S VOICE: Very.

BUCK: Great. Then what?

JOEY'S VOICE: Well, there's a sort of jutting-out place.

BUCK: I hear water.

JOEY'S VOICE: There's this stream.

BUCK: Coming out of the cliff?

JOEY'S VOICE: No, stupid.

BUCK: What's so stupid? Water can come out of a cliff.

JOEY'S VOICE: Well, this water doesn't. The cliff ends here. There's a sort of a gorge that runs back up there.

BUCK: Don't say, "There." Where? Left? Right?

JOEY'S VOICE: Left, stupid. Where else could it be?

BUCK: All right. Got you.

JOEY'S VOICE: I guess there's a waterfall up there somewhere.

BUCK: Left?

JOEY's VOICE: Right. I mean: yeah.

BUCK: I can hear it.

JOEY's VOICE: Goody for you.

BUCK: Then there's this stream.

JOEY's VOICE: Check.

BUCK: Running from left to right.

JOEY's VOICE: Now, you got it, baby.

BUCK: And what about this "jutting-out place"?

JOEY's VOICE: Well, it sort of juts out.

BUCK: A shelf.

JOEY's VOICE: You do have the words, don't you?

BUCK: Or promontory.

JOEY's VOICE: Now, you've got me.

BUCK: And the stream runs out along that?

JOEY's VOICE: Sort of cuts into it, you might say.

BUCK: I... I think I get the picture. Then what happens to it – to the stream? It must go somewhere.

JOEY's VOICE: It goes along this prom... this shelf, and then it drops off into... into the whatdoyoucallit?

BUCK: The abyss.

JOEY's VOICE: Check.

BUCK: Where we all go in the end.

JOEY's VOICE: Cut that, will you?

BUCK: There must be two waterfalls then. One coming down from the left; one going down on the right.

JOEY's VOICE: Check and double check.

BUCK: Perhaps that's the one I hear, the one on the right.

JOEY's VOICE: Could be.

BUCK: Or maybe I hear both.

JOEY's VOICE: Maybe both.

BUCK: Are you ready to go down?

JOEY's VOICE: My time is your time.

BUCK: Then down we go.

> BUCK's *feet start to descend the ladder. He falters after one step; stops.*

By God, it's steep.

JOEY's VOICE: Didn't I tell you?

BUCK: I don't think I can make it.

JOEY'S VOICE: Sure you can. We'll try the old trick: give me the pole.

BUCK: There you are.

JOEY'S VOICE: Got it.

The pole changes position as BUCK *hands the upper - and still invisible - end of it to* JOEY, *above him.*

Okay; easy does it… There… There.

BUCK *comes down a few steps, guiding himself by the pole, which* JOEY *is holding out in front of him.* JOEY'S *feet appear; he is riding on* BUCK'S *shoulders.*

BUCK: *(Stopping)* Just a minute.

JOEY: Now what?

BUCK: We get down to this stream; then what?

JOEY: We go across.

BUCK: How? Jump?

JOEY: Not with me on your back.

BUCK: Well?

JOEY: There's this bridge.

BUCK: Now you're talking. Why didn't you say so before?

JOEY: You didn't give me a chance.

BUCK: Sometimes I think you don't tell me everything.

JOEY: Look, are we going down? Or are we going to stand here while you run through that routine again?

BUCK: We're going down.

JOEY: Take hold of the stick.

BUCK *does so.*

Easy… Easy.

Slowly BUCK *descends with* JOEY. *Both become fully visible.* BUCK *carries a pack on his back.* JOEY *sits on it, with his legs over* BUCK'S *shoulders.*

BUCK: *(As he comes down)* It's true: you don't tell me everything.

JOEY: Shut up. Work now; talk later.

Pause. Another step.

BUCK: You're getting heavier.

JOEY: I am not.

BUCK: Well…

JOEY: Shut up. One more step, and we're down.… There.

THEY *have reached the bottom of the ladder.* JOEY *turns the pole over to* BUCK.

BUCK: Thank God for that! You <u>are</u> getting heavier.

HE *starts to go straight ahead, that is to say, towards stage left.*

JOEY: Now, where are you going?

BUCK: Over the bridge. Where else?

JOEY: But the bridge isn't there.

BUCK: What the fuck?

JOEY: Tisk, tsk, tsk! You do talk nice.

BUCK: I'll break your ass if you give me any more of that.

JOEY: It's breaking already. Have you got a fry-pan in this pack?

BUCK: You know I have a frying pan.

JOEY: Well, the handle's going right up the old wazoo.

BUCK: So somebody's getting a thrill.

JOEY: Thrill, hell. It's damned uncomfortable.

BUCK: You're damned uncomfortable.

JOEY: So we're quits.

BUCK: I know you've been putting on weight. You've been eating more than your share.

JOEY: Do you want to hear about this bridge?

BUCK: Please, tell me about the bridge.

JOEY: We turn right.

BUCK: Out onto the promontory.

JOEY: Right.

BUCK: And over the edge. Into the abyss.

JOEY: Will you cut that!

BUCK: It would be just like you to lead me off the edge.

JOEY: Sure, with me on your back.

BUCK: Okay; we turn right.

BUCK *turns right, that is, facing downstage.*

JOEY: That's the ticket.

BUCK: Now what?

JOEY: We go on a few feet and then turn left. That's where the bridge is.

BUCK: All right: we're off and running.

HE *starts to move.*

JOEY: Take it easy; there's all sorts of loose rock and crap along here.

BUCK: Loose rock? Where?

HE *stubs his toe.*

JOEY: There, for instance. Take it easy for Chrissake. Use your pole.

BUCK: How'm I doing?

JOEY: Fine, fine, fine. Now turn left and over we go.

BUCK: Over the edge?

JOEY: Over the bridge, you dumb fuck.

BUCK: Now who's talking dirty?

JOEY: Okay, so I ain't neat.

BUCK: *(Feeling with the pole)* Is this the bridge?

JOEY: You guessed it; you win the teddy bear.

BUCK: *(Stepping onto the "bridge")* I want to stop here.

JOEY: Further on it's nicer. It sort of flattens out, and there's some trees and a kind of open place.

BUCK: Graphic description.

JOEY: So you got the words; I do the best I can. We could have a picnic over there.

BUCK: I want to stop on the bridge. My feet are killing me; I want to dangle them in the water.

JOEY: You can't: the bridge is too far up; water's too far down.

BUCK: We're going to stop on the bridge.

JOEY: We're going to stop on the bridge.

BUCK: And you're getting off. Just for a while.

JOEY: Great place you picked for this act.

BUCK: *(Tipping* JOEY *off)* Off you get.

JOEY: Easy, man: you're sliding me into the drink.

BUCK: Sorry.

JOEY: *(Crawling off* BUCK'S *back and settling himself)* There now.

BUCK, *sitting on the edge of the "bridge", swings his feet over the edge.*

What are you doing?

BUCK: Dangling.

JOEY: What did I tell you?

BUCK: Check: bridge too far up; water too far down.

JOEY: Check.

BUCK: Now what? I've got to soak my feet.

JOEY: That's not all you should soak.

BUCK: Cut the comedy and tell me what to do.

JOEY: *(Prodding* BUCK*)* All right: inch along a little.

BUCK: *(Inching left on his hams)* Inching.

JOEY: Right. Now there's this little path, very narrow, very steep…

BUCK: *(Feeling about with his feet)* Little path, very narrow, very steep. Where?

JOEY: Just after the bridge, to your left. It leads down the bank to the water.

BUCK: *(Still searching)* Little path, very narrow...

JOEY: Look here: I'm pointing at it with the pole.

Taking the pole, he pokes it at the kitchen ladder.

BUCK: Where's the pole?

Feels for it; finds it.

Oh, got it!

JOEY: Feel along the pole and you'll find the path.

BUCK: *(Doing so)* Got it.

HE *starts to get up.*

JOEY: Don't try it standing up, you fool; you'll fall into the drink. Just scrunch along on your ass.

BUCK: Scrunching.

JOEY: Thatta baby!

BUCK *locates the ladder "path."*

BUCK: Ah!

Gropes his way onto the "path" and inches down a step.

How'm I doing?

JOEY: Fine. You can reach the water from there.

BUCK: Better take off my shoes.

HE *does so.*

JOEY: Keen idea.

BUCK: And my socks.

Takes off socks.

JOEY: Peachy keen.

BUCK: You'd better take them. Here.

JOEY: Don't try to throw them to me; hand them up.

BUCK: Handing.

JOEY: *(Taking shoes and socks)* Got 'em! Whew, they stink!

BUCK: Then stop smelling them, you damn fetishist.

JOEY: Yeah.

Seeing something.

What's that down there?

BUCK: What's what down where?

JOEY: Near your left foot. It's a bottle.

BUCK: What kind of bottle?

JOEY: How the hell should I know! Hand it up to me.

BUCK: *(Feeling about)* I've got to find it first.

JOEY: *(Prodding with the pole)* I'm poking at it with the pole.

BUCK: I'm so glad. All I've got to do is find the pole.

JOEY: Just reach for it.

BUCK: *(Reaching and finding it)* Got it!

>*Feeling along the pole; finding the bottle.*

>Bottle!

>*Examining the bottle with his hands.*

>Small bottle. Thought it might be booze.

JOEY: Maybe it is.

BUCK: *(Continuing examination)* More like a medicine bottle. There's a label on it.

JOEY: Hand it up; I'll read it to you.

BUCK: It says, "Drink me."

JOEY: Perhaps. Hand it up.

BUCK: Or maybe: "Poison."

JOEY: If it does, I'll let you know.

BUCK: Will you now?

JOEY: No: I'll let you drink the whole damn thing. Then push you over the edge and run off with your shoes.

BUCK: We understand each other.

JOEY: Good. Now give me the bottle.

BUCK: *(Handing it up)* Here.

JOEY: Got it. Cheez, there's a lot on this label. Small print.

BUCK: We're in trouble.

JOEY: I'll do my best. If you don't like it, you can read it yourself.

BUCK: Veddy funny; veddy funny. Go ahead: read.

JOEY: I've got problems already.

BUCK: Spell it.

JOEY: No, no: I'm making it. "Doctor Chol-mon-do-ley's..."

BUCK: That's "Chumlee".

JOEY: What?

BUCK: C.H.O.L.M.O.N.D.O.L.E.Y.: Chumlee.

JOEY: Have it your way. "Doctor Whatever's Miracle Water..."

BUCK: *(Contemptuously)* One of those things.

JOEY: Yes. Now, shut up: I'm reading.

BUCK: Go on.

JOEY: *(Making a brave start at a "poetic" recitation, but soon running into difficulties)* "A gentle, soothing tonic, effective for the relief of intestinal disorders and digestive irregularities, dyspepsia, flat-u-lence...". What the hell?

BUCK: Farting.

JOEY: What do you know? "Inflammation of the liver, morning sickness, constipation, nausea, diar..." Holy cow!

BUCK: Spell it.

JOEY: D.I.A.R.R.H.E.A.

BUCK: Diarrhea.

JOEY: Hell of a way to spell "rear".

BUCK: Go on.

JOEY: "Cardiac complaints, arterio-scler-osis, headache misery and colds' distress..."

BUCK: I knew it.

JOEY: "Diseases of the kidney and urinary tract, respiratory difficulties, neuralgia, arthritis or stiffening of the joints..." Well, what do you know: "paralysis!"

BUCK: *(Cynically)* You're in, boy.

JOEY: Hold on; maybe we'll get to you later.

BUCK: Not bloody likely.

JOEY: That's it: always look on the bright side.

BUCK: Go on.

JOEY: "Vitamin deficiencies, acne, pellagra, faulty vision..."

BUCK: That's putting it mildly.

JOEY: What did I tell you?

BUCK: Close, but no cigar.

JOEY: Wait. Here you are: the very next one: "Cataracts."

BUCK: Well, well, well. Something for everybody.

JOEY: You said it, baby.

Finishing with a flourish.

"Earache, dental caries, cancer, undulant fever, mononucleosis, artificial flavor and coloring added." Well, shall we have a bash?

BUCK: Are you out of your mind?

JOEY: Why?

BUCK: You're not going to drink that stuff?

JOEY: Why not?

BUCK: You don't know what's in it.

JOEY: Who gives a shit? Look what it cures.

BUCK: You'll believe anything, won't you?

JOEY: I'll try anything.

BUCK: Suppose it doesn't work?

JOEY: What have we got to lose?

He *uncorks the bottle; pause.*

BUCK: Suppose it does work.

JOEY: Aha!

BUCK: I mean...

JOEY: Suppose it works for me, but doesn't work for you?

BUCK: All right: suppose. What then?

JOEY: Easy. I give a little push. Over the edge you go, into the... ah... abyss. And I'm on my way. Free as a bird.

BUCK: *(Musing)* Free as a bird.

JOEY: Sure. No more use for poor old Buck when Joey walks by himself.

BUCK: Good riddance.

JOEY: For who?

BUCK: Both of us. We don't really get along together.

JOEY: That's the spirit! Want to risk it?

BUCK: Suit yourself.

JOEY: Come on, baby; cheer up. Joey's not going to leave you. You'll still have my eyes, and you won't have to carry me.

BUCK: It doesn't matter.

JOEY: You said I was getting heavier.

BUCK: Shut up, and drink the stuff.

JOEY: Maybe it's poison.

BUCK: Maybe it is.

JOEY: Aha!

He *drinks. Pause.*

BUCK: Well?

JOEY *pinches his left leg.* He *can feel the pinch. Takes another sip.*
Well?

JOEY *flexes his left leg, painfully. Pinches right leg. Reacts. Sips again.*
Are you dead?

JOEY: No.

Flexes right leg with greater difficulty.

BUCK: What's happening?

JOEY: Nothing much.

HE *can move his left leg quite freely; the right, almost as well. Great elation, suppressed.*

Put your hand out.

BUCK: Why?

JOEY: Put your hand out.

BUCK: *(Extending his right hand)* Like that?

JOEY: Like that.

With his left leg, he kick's BUCK'S *hand. Hard.*

BUCK: Hey, you kicked me!

JOEY: How do you like that?

BUCK: Holy Cow! It works!

JOEY: What do you know?

BUCK: *(Becoming excited)* Let me try it.

JOEY: Oho! You're interested!

BUCK: Damn right, I am.

JOEY: I'm just your little taster. Eh?

BUCK: Come off it.

JOEY: Okay for me to be your guinea pig, huh?

BUCK: *(Becoming angry)* For fuck sake, will you let me try it!

JOEY: Oh, ho, ho!

BUCK: *(Flailing about)* God damn you!

JOEY: Easy does it, or over you go; and I won't even have to push.

BUCK: *(Blind fury)* Aaaah!

JOEY: *(Scared)* All right already. Hold on; I'm giving it to you.

BUCK: *(Calming down; sullen)* I'll bet you drank it all.

JOEY: *(Holding out the bottle towards* BUCK*)* See for yourself.

BUCK *takes it. Sips. Pause.*

Leave some for me.

BUCK: *(Covering one eye with his hand; squinting with the other)* What the hell, you've had your share.

JOEY: The other leg isn't so hot.

HE *tests his right leg; it is almost perfect.*

BUCK: *(Skeptically)* Hmmm.

HE *sips again. Stretches both eyes open wide. The glare makes them smart.*
HE *shields them with his free hand. Sips again. Still squinting, he is able to
get up, walk about, very tentatively.*

JOEY: I said: leave some for me.

BUCK: *(Bellowing)* I'm leaving you some.

JOEY: Dear, dear. Such an angry one.

HE *rises and walks about on the "bridge" and platform, right. His right leg
is stiff at first, but improves with each step.* BUCK, *meanwhile, is preoccupied
with testing his vision with intermittent sips from the bottle.* HE *looks out, up,
and left, not towards* JOEY, *still absorbed by his walking exercises.*

Well?

Pause. Stopping; looking over towards BUCK.

Well?

BUCK: Hold your water.

JOEY: *(Coming over to* BUCK*)* Works, eh?

BUCK: I'm finding out now.

JOEY: Didn't believe it would, did you?

BUCK: Shut up.

*Covering his right eye, he is able to see easily out of his left without squint-
ing.*

Jesus Christ.

JOEY: My turn now.

BUCK: Shut up!

HE *covers his left eye; sees easily out of his right.*

JOEY: What are you doing?

BUCK: Testing.

Uncovers both eyes; sees perfectly.

Jesus Christ.

JOEY: Okay?

BUCK: Okay!

*Noticing his shoes and socks, he sits down and starts putting them on, leaving
the bottle on the "bridge" beside him, away from* JOEY.

JOEY: My turn now. Come on: just a sip for the old right leg.

BUCK: Get it yourself; I'm putting on my shoes.

JOEY: Your big ass is in the way.

Pause. BUCK *finishes putting on shoes and socks.*

Come on, Buck; don't be a complete bastard.

BUCK: Oh, for fuck sake, take it, take it, take it!

HE *takes up the bottle, thrusts it towards* JOEY, *splashing him.*

JOEY: Hey, watch what you're doing! Goddamn, right in the eye!

BUCK: I'm sorry. You were bugging me.

JOEY: It stings.

BUCK: *(Rising. Quite penitent. Takes handkerchief from his pocket)* Here: take this. Wipe.

JOEY: *(Taking handkerchief; wiping his eyes)* Damn; it stings.

BUCK: I'm sorry. Can you see all right?

JOEY: I can see all right.

Pause

Well, sort of all right.

BUCK: Jesus, Joey; your eyes are all red.

JOEY: What do you know!

BUCK: They're streaming.

JOEY: That stuff stings. Come on, let's go.

HE *is blinking; evidently in trouble.*

BUCK: Are you all right?

JOEY: I'll be all right.

BUCK: You don't look all right.

JOEY: I'll be all right. Come on.

Rubs his eyes.

BUCK: Stop rubbing them.

JOEY: What do you want me to do? It stings.

BUCK: Tie the handkerchief around them.

JOEY: Huh?

BUCK: *(Grabbing the handkerchief from* JOEY; *blindfolding him)* Like this, stupid.

JOEY: Great. I can't see anything now.

BUCK: You couldn't see anything before.

JOEY: Of course, I could.

BUCK: Then what were you bitching about?

JOEY: I only said my eyes stung. They hurt. I didn't say anything about not seeing.

HE *tears off the blindfold.*

There. I can see fine now.

HE *obviously can.*

BUCK: But they still hurt, no? They look awful.

JOEY: *(After a pause. Reluctantly)* They still hurt, yes. But not so much.

BUCK: Then put the bandage on. Just for a while. To rest them.

JOEY: But…

BUCK: Here, give me that.

HE *snatches the handkerchief from* JOEY *and forcibly ties it about his eyes.*

JOEY: What the hell!

BUCK: It's only temporary.

JOEY: *(Giving in)* Okay, now what am I supposed to do?

BUCK: Don't worry; I'll lead you.

JOEY: *(Sarcastically)* Great.

BUCK: It's only temporary. Come on.

Takes up the pole.

JOEY: Just a sec while I get my bearings.

Feels about with his foot.

Bridge.

BUCK: Yeah.

JOEY: Good. Now we're all squared away.

Pointing in all the wrong directions.

Open place, that way. Trees, over there. Cliff, back up that way. Down there: abyss.

BUCK: You think so?

JOEY: For Chrissake, stop the horse-shit. Am I right or wrong?

BUCK: Just keep on the way you're going.

JOEY: Okay.

HE *starts off right, the way they have come.*

BUCK: Right over the edge

JOEY: *(Stopping short)* You fucking son of a bitch! What a barrel of laughs.

BUCK: Now you see what it's like.

JOEY: Yuck, yuck!

BUCK: Reach out your hand.

JOEY: What are you up to now?

BUCK: Come on. You can trust me.

JOEY: *(Skeptically)* Sure.

BUCK: Come on. Give me your hand. Stop waving it about.

JOEY: *(Reaching in* BUCK's *direction)* Where are you?

BUCK: *(Taking* JOEY's *hand)* There. Now, take it easy. Let me guide you.

JOEY: Fine mess this is.

BUCK: Stop complaining. It could be worse. Take hold of my belt.

Moves JOEY'S *hand behind him to his belt.*

There.

THEY *start down the ramp, left.*

JOEY: Where are you taking me?

BUCK: Down. Slowly now; it's kind of steep.

JOEY: Down where?

BUCK: To the sylvan glade.

JOEY: Whaaat?

BUCK: Open place.

Reaches the bottom of the ramp.

Here we are.

JOEY: Let's have a picnic.

BUCK: No. There's a path off through the trees. It's easy all the way.

JOEY: How can you tell?

BUCK: I can see.

To himself.

I can see.

JOEY: I'm hungry.

BUCK: We'll be at the bottom in no time.

JOEY: *(Musing)* The bottom of the abyss.

BUCK: When you fall into it, it's an abyss. When you walk there, it's just a valley.

JOEY: I'm still hungry.

BUCK: And I'm tired; but we're going on.

JOEY: Your feet must hurt.

BUCK: Something awful. Come.

HE *starts off, up left.*

JOEY: *(Stopping him)* Wait a minute.

BUCK: What now?

JOEY: You've done all the walking; I haven't done any.

BUCK: So?

JOEY: I'll carry you.

BUCK: Don't be an ass.

JOEY: I can do it. For a while anyway. You said your feet hurt.

BUCK: Not that much. Come on.

JOEY: Not unless I carry you.

BUCK: Joey. Make sense.

JOEY: *(Adamant)* Onto my back.

BUCK: *(Affectionately)* You stupid fuck.

JOEY: Onto my back.

BUCK: Oh well. But only temporary. Take the pole.

JOEY: *(Taking it)* Only temporary. Climb on.

BUCK: Squat down a little.

JOEY: Squatting.

BUCK: Okay.

> HE *climbs onto* JOEY'S *back.*

JOEY: Oof!

> *Settling* BUCK *into position.*

> So: off we go. Where?

BUCK: *(Pointing up left)* There.

JOEY: Right or left, you bastard. Who knows where "there" is?

BUCK: Left.

> JOEY *turns sharply upstage.*

> Not too much.

> JOEY *turns a bit to his right.*

> That's it.

JOEY: Off and running.

> *Starting off.*

BUCK: Take it easy now; look out for the trees.

JOEY: I can manage.

BUCK: Yeah.

> THEY *go off, up left, through the "trees."*

> Now where are you going?

JOEY'S VOICE: *(Off left)* What do mean: where am I going?

BUCK'S VOICE: One step more and you're into the bush.

JOEY'S VOICE: *(More distant)* Oh.

BUCK'S VOICE: *(Distant)* A bit to your right now. No, goddamn it, can't you tell right from left . . .

> *The voices fade off left. Pause. Silence. Empty stage.*

THE CURTAIN FALLS

www.ingramcontent.com/pod-product-compliance
Lightning Source LLC
Chambersburg PA
CBHW031301090426
42742CB00007B/547